Hawaiian Monarchs and Their Palaces™

(A Pictorial History)

A condensed pictorial history of Hawaii's monarchs, beginning with Kamehameha the Great, the founder of the Hawaiian Kingdom, and ending with Queen Lili'uokalani, the last Hawaiian monarch.

Compiled, Written, and Edited by:

Richard A. Wisniewski

Designed and Arranged by:

Herbert Goeas

Printed in Honolulu, Hawaii by:

Pacific Printers, Inc.

●

Published and Distributed by:

Pacific Basin Enterprises
P.O. Box 8924
Honolulu, Hawaii 96830

Table of Contents

Introduction

Historians generally agree that the first settlers to the Hawaiian Islands arrived sometime around 800 to 900 A.D. These early Polynesians were part of a continuing eastward migration into the Pacific that had started tens of thousands of years ago from the various islands of Southeast Asia. Whether these early voyagers were forced to migrate because of warfare or food-supply problems, or whether they migrated out of a spirit of adventure, the fact remains that their journeys covered great distances and often opposed the prevailing direction of trade winds and ocean currents. These skilled navigators and daring adventurers often used chants to orally pass on the knowledge that they had learned about the wind, ocean currents, and the stars. Historians also believe that these first settlers to Hawaii, who had traveled in large double-hulled canoes, came from Tahiti or islands near Tahiti because ancient chants and legends contain names which identify with islands in this region.

The ancient Hawaiian civilization was a feudal system which consisted of a highly cultivated upper class supported by an underprivileged lower class. The highest authority resided with the king (ali'i 'ai moku or ali'i nui), and he had absolute authority over all his subjects. A chief minister (Kālaimoku or Kalanimoku) organized and administered the political system and looked out for the interests of the common people. A high priest (kahuna nui) conducted the important religious ceremonies and advised the king so that he would retain the favor of the gods. The chiefs (ali'i) ruled over sections of land that the king had bestowed upon them. The kahunas were craftsmen/priests who specialized in various professions. And the common people, who made up the largest portion of the population and lived in subjugation to the chief upon whose land they lived, were called maka'āinana. Kauwā were the outcasts. The kapu (tabu) system regulated the daily lives of the people and insured the continuation of the class system.

Throughout the centuries, wars were commonplace, usually arising out of disputes over succession or territory. Famine, death, and destruction accompanied these wars, causing much suffering among the people. But not all of Hawaii's past ali'i were warlords. Some ruled with wisdom and compassion. Others like 'Umi, brought justice to their people. Lono introduced reforms in religion and government and used competitive games as a substitute for warfare. Yet throughout these centuries of warfare, no single individual could unite all the islands into one kingdom until Kamehameha the Great accomplished that feat in the nineteenth century. Among all of Hawaii's chiefs, Kamehameha has been recognized as the most outstanding. The kingdom that he founded, and the continued existence of that kingdom for nearly a hundred years make up the subject matter of this publication. It is by no means a complete story; rather, it seeks to introduce the reader to Hawaii's recent monarchs and to entice him (or her) into further exploring and researching their histories.

The Hawaiian Language

Since the Hawaiians didn't have a written language, early visitors to the islands attempted to write down the names of various Hawaiian people and places. But these early attempts resulted in different spellings. Realizing that education was the key to "winning" over the natives, the missionaries reduced the Hawaiian language to an easily understood and useable form. Eliminating all silent letters, and attempting to avoid arbitrary spellings, ambiguities, and inconsistencies, they assigned a certain character to a certain sound, thereby deriving a true Hawaiian pronunciation. The resulting alphabet consisted of twelve letters — five vowels and seven consonants. While slight variations and exceptions exist, the following simplified guide will help the reader in pronouncing Hawaiian words.

Pronunciation of vowels:

a, as the "a" in father
e, as the "ey" in they
i, as the "ee" in see

o, as the "o" in no
u, as the "oo" in too

Most vowels are pronounced separately, and the full accent is usually placed on the second to the last vowel. However, numerous exceptions do exist to these rules. For example, "ae" and "ai" are frequently spoken as an "i" (eye), and "oe" and "oi" are often pronounced as the "oy" in boy. Other double-vowel combinations such as "ao," "au," "ei," "eu" and "ou" generally come together as a diphthong. Unless a glottal stop (') separates the two vowels, they are usually slurred together with the second vowel being light or unaccented. The glottal stop signifies a short break or pause, and a macron (ˉ) placed above a vowel indicates a somewhat longer (stressed) sound. The presence or absence of these marks can change both the pronunciation and meaning of the word. A good example is the Hawaiian word pau (pow). Standing alone, pau means done or finished; but pa'u (pa-oo) means soot or smudge, pa'ū (pa-OO) means damp or moist, and pāʻū (PA-OO) means a woman's sarong or long skirt.

Pronunciation of consonants:

Nearly all the consonants (h, k, l, m, n, p, and w) are pronounced about the same as they are in English. The "w" is an exception because it is sometimes pronounced as a "v" due to variations in local custom. This is especially true if the "w" follows an "i" or an "e". If it follows an "a" or is the first letter of a word, then it can be either a "w" or a "v" — Waikiki (Why-KEE-KEE').[1]

Sample pronunciations:

ISLANDS[1]	PEOPLE
Hawai'i (Ha-why'-ee)	Ka'ahumanu (Ka-a-hoo-ma'-noo)
Kahoolawe (Ka-ho-o'-la-vey)	Kalākaua (Ka-LA-kow'-wa)
Kaua'i (Ka-wah'-ee)	Kamehameha (Ka-mey-ha-mey'-ha)
Lāna'i (LA-nah'-ee)	Kauikeaouli (Kow-ee-kay-(a)ow(o)-oo'-lee)
Maui (Mow'-wee)	Liholiho (Lee-ho-lee'-ho)
Moloka'i (Mo-lo-kah'-ee)	Lili'uokalani (Li-lee-oo-o-ka-la'nee)
Ni'ihau (Nee-ee'-how)	Lunalilo (Loo-na-lee'-lo)
O'ahu (O-wah'-hoo)	

---

[1] These pronunciations are based on the established usage by native speakers. However, in actual usage today, the glottal stops and macrons are frequently omitted, and the "ai" double vowels in Kauai, Lanai, and Molokai are often slurred together as an "i" (eye). So as not to confuse the first-time reader, the author has intentionally omitted these punctuation marks for the islands and Waikiki.

CHAPTER 1

Kamehameha, the Great: The Warrior King

Tamehameha[2] in the 1790's by Herb Kawainui Kane

Artist's Collection

Ka'ahumanu by Herb Kawainui Kane

Artist's Collection

KAMEHAMEHA[1]
BORN: c. 1758
FATHER: Keōua Kalanikupuapā, a half brother of Kalani-'ōpu'u (King of Hawaii)
MOTHER: Keku'i'apoiwa, a niece of Kahekili (King of Maui)
RULED: 1795 until his death on May 8, 1819

KA'AHUMANU (Favorite Wife)
BORN: c. 1768
FATHER: Ke'eaumoku, a renowned warrior and counselor to Kamehameha
MOTHER: Nāmāhana, a chiefess of Maui
DIED: June 5, 1832

According to Hawaiian legends, Kamehameha was born in Kohala on the island of Hawaii probably in 1758. These legends stated that thunder, lightning, and a strange light in the heavens with the tail feathers of a bird announced the birth of

---

[1] 1758 is his probable birth date that many historians accept. Yet dates as early as 1736 and as late as 1761 have been offered. There is also disagreement over his parentage — a Hawaiian tradition asserts that his father was Kahekili, the Maui king. References to a strange light in the heavens might refer to Halley's Comet which would have been visible in Hawaiian skies in November or December of 1758. Following the custom of all great chiefs, Kamehameha took many wives and had many offspring.

[2] This is the old spelling before the missionaries adopted a common alphabet and substituted a "k" for a "t" since these consonants were sometimes interchangeable in speech.

the baby who was destined to become a great chief. His father was the chief of Kohala and a grandson of Keawe who once ruled over a powerful kingdom on Hawaii. His mother was the daughter of a Kona chief.

Immediately after his birth, the child was taken away and hidden to protect him from possible death at the hands of warring clans. Originally named Pai'ea, Kamehameha spent five years hidden in the secluded valley of Waipi'o, a sanctuary to endangered ali'i (royalty). After the death threat passed, he was returned to his parents. Old Chief Alapa'i, who had initiated the death threat, now accepted Pai'ea and named him Kamehameha ("The Lonely One"). For about the next seven years, he received the care and training that was reserved only for the ali'i.

At about the age of fourteen, Kamehameha's father died, and his uncle, King Kalani'ōpu'u, adopted him. Treated as a son, Kamehameha relocated to the district of Ka'ū, domain of the fire-goddess Pele on the snow-rimmed slopes of Mauna Loa. Here a special breed of Hawaiians resided — proud, independent, and fierce in battle. Under the careful tutelage of a very great warrior, Kamehameha learned spear throwing and dodging, wrestling, and the rudimentary tactics of warfare. Here also, his sexual urges were satisfied with carefully selected young women. Without a written language, Kamehameha learned navigation, astronomy, history, his genealogy, religious ceremonies, prayers and kapus (tabus), and other vital information necessary for him to become a district chief. As his training progressed, his physical aptitudes became unmatched.

Captain James Cook, Royal Navy

At this time, continuous warfare, interrupted by brief periods of peace, ravaged the islands. Also at this time, the outside world discovered the Hawaiian Islands.[1] On the morning of January 18, 1778, Captain James Cook and the ships of his Third Voyage (*Resolution* and *Discovery*) sighted first Oahu and then Kauai. Anchoring at Waimea on the western side of Kauai, Cook and his landing parties were treated with awe. He had arrived during the makahiki season, a festive season in which taxes were collected, people rested from the labors of the harvest, and war was forbidden. The news of the strange visitors spread quickly to the other islands. When Cook's ships again appeared in Hawaiian waters, first off the coast of Maui in late November of 1778 and again in Kealakekua Bay off the island of Hawaii in January of 1779, Cook was greeted with the same curiosity and respect.

---

[1] References to other foreigners reaching these islands appear in Hawaiian legends. Also, it is claimed that the Spanish navigator Juan Gaetano may have discovered them in 1555 while sailing between Mexico and the Philippines. But in both cases, insufficient proof exists to satisfy historians.

By now, Kamehameha was an experienced warrior — tall, strong, and fearless. He moved with an aura of power and violence. Having accompanied his uncle, King Kalani'ōpu'u, aboard the *Discovery,* Kamehameha was obviously impressed with Cook's warriors and their guns and iron weapons. After Cook's death (February 14, 1779), legends say that Kamehameha further added to his mana (power and prestige) by claiming and keeping Cook's hair.[1] Returning to his home district of Kohala, Kamehameha bided his time. He was still there when his uncle died in 1782. Following the death of this important chief, the rule over his lands passed to his son, Kīwala'ō, the senior heir. Kamehameha now took control of Kū (Kūka'ilimoku), the war god — a feathery image with a mouth full of sharp teeth.

The Death of Captain Cook — Drawing by John Weber

Kīwala'ō took control of his father's kingdom by forming an alliance with his uncle (Keawema'uhili) and his younger brother (Keōua). At a place called Moku-'ōhai in mid-1782, they did battle with Kamehameha's forces. Kīwala'ō was killed, and Kamehameha now became a major contester for power. Four years of continuous warfare followed, yet the island of Hawaii remained divided into three kingdoms. In the meantime, Kahekili of Maui had taken control of Oahu. By 1786, it looked as though he might unite all the islands. He ruled the kingdom of Maui (which included Molokai and Lanai); he was now all powerful on Oahu; and he made an agreement with his brother (Ka'eokulani) on Kauai.

As a result of Cook's discoveries along the northwest coast of America, a new fur trade developed between these hunting grounds and their market in China. Requiring a rendezvous point to replenish their exhausted supplies of food and fresh water, these traders began calling at the Sandwich[2] (Hawaiian) Islands. In 1786, four foreign ships visited the islands, and each year thereafter, one or more ships anchored in Hawaiian waters. Between 1786 and 1790, relative peace prevailed. But the Hawaiian chiefs used his time to supply themselves with new weapons that they acquired from the foreigners.

Early in 1790, Kamehameha's warriors captured the schooner *Fair American* after killing the ship's crew in retaliation for a previous, unrelated incident. Kamehameha took possession of the schooner and its lone survivor, Isaac Davis. He also

---

[1] Perhaps overstaying his welcome, Cook and his ships left Kealakekua Bay on February 4, 1779. Caught in a storm several days later, the squadron returned on the 11th because of a damaged foremast. While repairs were under way, the natives resumed their petty thievery to obtain iron. A major showdown occurred on the 14th over a stolen cutter. In the ensuing scuffle, Cook and four marines were killed. The Hawaiians treated Cook's body like one of their own chiefs.

[2] Cook named the island chain in honor of his patron, John Montagu, Fourth Earl of Sandwich and First Lord of the Admiralty.

put another prisoner named John Young under his protection. Gradually adjusting to their fate, Young and Davis taught Kamehameha's warriors how to use the cannon and muskets aboard the schooner. They coached the king on western customs and taught him new tricks in trading with the foreigners. Given wives, land, and the equivalent status of chiefs, Young and Davis eventually became Kamehameha's confidential advisors. With their help, the ambitious king equipped an army, Anglo-style, and a navy that included an immense fleet of shallow-draft and double-hulled canoes in addition to the cannon-rigged *Fair American.*

Learning that Kahekili was trying to put down a full-fledged revolt on Oahu, Kamehameha made plans to assault Maui. He consulted the kahunas (priests), built new heiaus (temples), and received pledges of canoes, warriors, and supplies from his chiefs. He even won the friendship and support of a former enemy, Keawe. Kamehameha's enormous fleet beached near Hāna and worked its way along the northern coast to assault Wailuku. Along the way, he picked up supplies and won support for his cause from many of the local chiefs. At a small hill called Pu'uko'a, Kamehameha's forces defeated a large army sent by the Maui king's son, Kalanikupule.

'Iao Valley, Maui

Hawaii Visitors Bureau

Kamehameha now moved his forces to Wailuku for the major confrontation. As they arrived, the bay filled with war canoes. When the large brass cannon arrived with its specially constructed wheels and more than eighty attendants to move, load, and fire it, Kamehameha started the battle. After two days of constant fighting, the defenders were pushed up against the narrow pass of the 'Iao Valley. At this point, Kamehameha ordered the brass cannon to be fired into the valley, thereby routing the defenders. His superior forces aggressively pursued the defenders and a great slaughter took place — so much so, that the bodies of the dead warriors filled the stream and stopped the flow of water. But all the important chiefs managed to escape.

After his conquest of Maui, Kamehameha went to Molokai where he took into his care his step-mother's daughter (Keōpūolani), a very high-ranking ali'i. Because Ka'ahumanu could not produce any children for him, Kamehameha later chose Keōpūolani to become another of his wives. While still on Molokai, Kamehameha sent his favorite wife's grandmother to search for a renowned soothsayer who could provide divine guidance. She found him at a stop in Waikiki. Being a cousin, he told her that in order for Kamehameha to rule over all the islands, he would have to build a great heiau for the war god Kū at Pu'ukoholā. If Kamehameha did as the seer envisioned, he would gain the kingdom.

Meanwhile, Kamehameha received the bad news that his rival on Hawaii (Keōua) had killed his recent ally (Keawe). Returning home, Kamehameha engaged his rival in two bloody, but inconclusive battles. Both sides then withdrew to their own territories to regroup. In November of 1790, a sudden eruption of Kīlauea Volcano destroyed part of Keōua's forces. Kamehameha and his kahunas interpreted this event as a positive omen, and they set out to build the prophesized heiau. Thousands of workers, chiefs of high and low rank, and even Kamehameha himself carried stones for the walls and platform of the heiau. Upon completion, it resembled a fortress. Shortly thereafter, a minor battle took place, and Keōua and most of his attendants were killed. Keōua's body was sacrificed at Pu'ukoholā, thereby fulfilling the prophecy. Thus in 1791, the island of Hawaii came under the undisputed rule of Kamehameha.

Keōua Arriving at Kawaihae, the Moment Before His Death[1] — by Herb Kawainui Kane

National Park Service Collection

These senseless power struggles devastated the economy of the islands so much that Kamehameha rested for several years. Thus a period of peace prevailed from 1791 to about the summer of 1794. During this calm, the Hawaiian chiefs continued to acquire foreign weapons, skills, and advisors. Many of the traders openly encouraged this rivalry, selling guns and ammunition to both sides. But the intentions of a British explorer named George Vancouver were more honorable and peaceful. As a junior officer, Vancouver had accompanied Captain Cook on both of his visits to Hawaii. Now as commander of an official exploring expedition, he sought to associate the islands with the British empire. Vancouver visited all the islands, met with all the important chiefs, and maintained friendly relations with them. Recognizing Kamehameha's superior position, Vancouver cultivated a special friendship with him and even tried, unsuccessfully, to conclude a peace treaty between Kamehameha and his rivals.

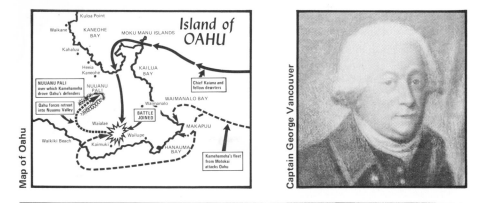

Map of Oahu

Captain George Vancouver

[1] The fortress-like Pu'ukoholā Heiau is in the background.

During the summer of 1794, several months after Vancouver's departure, the aged Maui King (Kahekili) died at Waikiki. His kingdom was then divided up between his brother (Ka'eo) and his son (Kalanikupule). Within a short time, these two chiefs drifted into war with each other. The forces of Kalanikupule prevailed after Ka'eo was killed in a battle fought in mid-December of 1794. Arrogant with victory, the surviving chief made plans to attack Kamehameha on the island of Hawaii.

Chief Ka'iana – Drawing by John Webber

Author's Collection

Warned of Kalanikupule's hostile intentions, Kamehameha was already preparing a huge army and a fleet of canoes. With over 16,000 men plus cannon, guns, and the technical knowledge of Young and Davis, Kamehameha attacked Maui, destroyed Lahaina, and ravaged the western side of the island. Capturing Molokai with little resistance, he proceeded on to Oahu. Despite a desertion by part of his army led by Chief Ka'iana, Kamehameha landed his well-seasoned forces at Waikiki in April of 1795. In the Nu'uanu Valley, the Oahu defenders made a stand. The ensuing battle was fierce, and the defenders gave ground only after many chiefs and warriors died. The survivors either fled into the mountains or were pushed over the steep cliffs of the Pali to find death on the rocks far below.[1] Others, fearing torture and sacrifice if captured, chose death by jumping into the deep crevasse below.

Kalanikupule managed to escape, but Kamehameha's forces found the fugitive king several months later and sacrificed him to Kū at a heiau at Moanalua. After his decisive victory, Kamehameha remained on Oahu to complete the pacification of the islands and to prepare for the conquest of Kauai and Niihau. In the spring of 1796, an attempted invasion of Kauai failed because strong winds and high seas suddenly arose and swamped many canoes.

Kamehameha had to return to Hawaii to put down a rebellion that was started by Namakeha, Ka'iana's brother. Taking the young chiefs along with him lest they become power hungry in his absence, Kamehameha left mostly trusted commoners in charge and returned to Hawaii in September to re-establish his supremacy. The main battle took place at Hilo, and Kamehameha's superior forces crushed the revolt. Although Namakeha managed to escape, he was later captured and sacrificed to Kū in early 1797.

While Kauai remained a thorn in his side, this battle at Hilo would be the final battle for Kamehameha. He remained on Hawaii for about six years. There, he

---

[1]See the back cover of this publication for a re-creation of this famous battle by Hawaiian artist Herb Kawainui Kane.

administered his kingdom, rewarded his loyal followers with gifts of land, and encouraged peaceful activities among his people. Yet during these years of peace, Kamehameha planned for the conquest of Kauai. To this end, he had his chiefs construct peleleu war canoes. These canoes were actually two large canoes that had been lashed together. Equipped with a mast and sails, they would be seaworthy enough to withstand the stormy channel between Kauai and Oahu. In addition to this 800-plus peleleu fleet, Kamehameha also had his foreign carpenters build a squadron of small schooners.

By the spring of 1804, Kamehameha had moved his huge armada to Oahu. But a terrible pestilence suddenly struck before he could launch his invasion. Called 'oku'u,[1] it spread quickly, decimating the population and killing many prime warriors and chiefs. It even struck Kamehameha, but he managed to survive its death grip. As a result of this pestilence, the invasion was postponed and the peleleu fleet rotted in the hot Hawaiian sun.

But despite this setback, Kamehameha was still intent on bringing Kauai into his kingdom. So he continued making plans and again began assembling a navy, this time patterned after the foreign ships. Although a number of attempts at reaching a peace agreement had been tried by both Kamehameha and the Kauai king, now Kaumuali'i (son of Ka'eo), distrust kept the Kauai king from going to Oahu. However, in 1810, an American trader named Captain Nathan Winship finally persuaded Kaumuali'i to go with him to Honolulu and arrange a truce. Meeting face to face, the two kings settled their differences; Kauai became a tributary kingdom that Kaumuali'i would continue to rule. In return, the Kauai king would acknowledge Kamehameha as his sovereign, thereby making Kamehameha the undisputed ruler of the kingdom.

In the early years of Kamehameha's kingdom, he had a body of advisors who in effect acted as a council of state. Because of their power and assistance in aiding Kamehameha in his long struggle for supremacy, these chiefs were almost always

---

[1] 'Oku'u means to squat. This disease might have been dysenteric cholera.

consulted before decisions on   important matters could be made. But as these chiefs died and their sons replaced them, their influence on Kamehameha diminished and his authority became absolute.

Kamehameha appointed a young chief named Kalanimoku to act as his executive officer. Actually, the name was more of a title since this young chief adopted the name William Pitt after his contemporary, the English prime minister. Kamehameha also appointed governors to be his representatives on each of the other islands, except for Kauai. The kapu system continued as a code of law. Its power of life and death held the nation together since it touched every facet of Hawaiian life. The prohibitions and restrictions of the kapus constantly reminded the people of the presence of their gods; and since the ali'i were believed to be descendants of these gods, many of the kapus referred directly to them. The penalties for violating the kapus were severe; often the victim was clubbed or strangled to death or he was killed in some other gruesome way and offered as a sacrifice on a heiau. While these kapus were often oppressive, the Hawaiian people remained intensely loyal to their leaders just as they had done for centuries.

Kamehameha I by James Gay Sawkins

Kamehameha continued to reside on Oahu until the summer of 1812 when he returned to Kona. Peace prevailed during this time, and Kamehameha spent much of his time fishing, rebuilding heiaus, and attending to agricultural production. Although Kamehameha was ruthless in war, he could be kind and forgiving when the need arose. While he appreciated the advantages offered by the foreigners, he never fell into their power. His good judgment and strong will prevailed. Through constant vigilance and internal strength, Kamehameha held his kingdom together until the last days of his life. That end came on the eighth day of May in 1819 when the great king succumbed to a long illness.

As word of the king's death reached the people, a great grief fell upon them. With the exception of human sacrifice, which Kamehameha had forbidden on his deathbed, the people observed the old customs for their departed king. At the appropriate time, the king's bones were carefully hidden, and their location has never been revealed to this day.

CHAPTER 2

Kamehameha, II: The Adventurous King

Portrait of Kamehameha II by John Hayter

Portrait of Kamāmalu by John Hayter

KALANI KUA LIHOLIHO

BORN: c. 1797
FATHER: Kamehameha the Great
MOTHER: Keōpūolani, the highest-
           ranking wife of Kamehameha
RULED: May 20, 1819 until his death
           on July 14, 1824

KAMĀMALU

BORN: c. 1802
FATHER: Kamehameha the Great
MOTHER: Kalakua (also called
           Kaheiheimalie), a wife of
           Kamehameha I
DIED: July 8, 1824

Following the death of his famous father, Liholiho fled to Kohala until the Kailua area could be ceremoniously cleansed. About a week later, he returned for his formal inauguration. Wearing an English red suit with gold trim, a feather helmet, and a feather cloak over his shoulders, Liholiho presented himself to his people. Ka'ahumanu, the royal guardian, presided over the ceremony. In her final statement, Ka'ahumanu stated that she would share the rule over the land with the new king. Liholiho consented, thereby becoming Kamehameha II.

In claiming to echo the last words of her deceased husband, Ka'ahumanu created for herself a new position in the government — that of kuhina nui. In effect, she became the executive officer. Whether the late king had wanted her to have this new power or whether she usurped it, the fact remained that no one challenged her authority. The new king was young (about 22); he had a reputation as a gambler and a playboy; and he had a craving for whiskey. With these shortcomings, Liholiho would need the guidance of a firm hand and Ka'ahumanu undoubtedly felt that she could provide that guidance. In accordance with the last wishes of Kamehameha I, Kekuaokalani, Liholiho's cousin, received custody of Kū (the war god).

With the rule of the land now divided between Liholiho and Ka'ahumanu, and with the custody of Kū no longer in possession of the person who also ruled the land, the prediction of a well-known German naturalist named Adelbert von Chamisso[1] seemed about to come true: " . . . after the death of the old hero, his kingdom, founded and kept together by force, will fall to pieces, the partition of it already decided upon, and prepared."

Kalani Kua Liholiho ("Heaven's Great Glowing") was raised during peacetime. Adored and spoiled, he led a sheltered life and grew up in luxury. At the age of five, his father proclaimed him successor to the throne. Although coached in warfare, Liholiho commanded no troops, fought in no battles, and never ruled over an island or a district before becoming king.

Three Chiefs of the Hawaiian Islands[2] — Drawing by Pellion

Liholiho ascended the throne at a time when foreign influences, material possessions, and new standards and ideas were propelling the Hawaiians into the modern, western world. Unknown diseases devastated the population, and traditional values and practices were increasingly being questioned by the people. The new king had acquired four high-born wives, and his third wife, Kamāmalu, was his half sister and his favorite. Thrust into greatness under the shadow of his mighty father, Liholiho often escaped from reality by drinking, gambling, and seeking other pleasures. Early in his reign, still unsure of his powers, he could not resist the pressures of the ruling chiefs to share in the royal sandalwood monopoly.

Shortly after Liholiho's inauguration, Ka'ahumanu let the new king know of her intention to end the kapu that segregated the sexes at meal time. Obtaining the allegiance of the queen mother, Ka'ahumanu put mounting pressure on the new king until he finally gave in. During a great feast in early November of 1819, the king, who had been imbibing heavily in rum, sat at an empty chair at the women's table, thereby breaking the eating kapu. When the meal was finished, the

---

[1]Chamisso made this statement between 1816 and 1817 after Kamehameha had proclaimed Liholiho as his successor and had named a new custodian for Kū. Chamisso accompanied Lt. Otto von Kotzebue of the Russian Imperial Navy who commanded the *Rurick*.

[2]Cox Ke'eaumoku, Governor of Maui and the son of Ke'eaumoku who was commander-in-chief of Kamehameha's forces in all his war campaigns, is in the center. One of his principal officers is on the right. The chief on the left, with the tatoo mourning the death of Kamehameha the Great, is Hoapili, guardian of the princess Nahi'ena'ena (Kamehameha's daughter) and husband of Keōpūolani (Kamehameha's wife).

king ordered the destruction of the heiaus (temples) and the burning of the idols.

Wooden Idols at the Reconstructed Hale o Keawe Temple in the Pu'uhonua o Hōnaunau National Historical Park

Photo by Author

Although a revolt broke out over the sudden abolition of the kapus, the king's army easily crushed it. Actually, this overthrow had been slowly developing for many years. Foreigners openly violated the kapus ashore and they went unpunished. Natives, who returned from visits to foreign lands, boasted about violating the kapus and suffering no apparent harm. Also, the kapu system in Tahiti had been overturned recently, so pressures for its overthrow in Hawaii had been mounting for some time. Finally, many chiefs supported the abolition since it would allow them to amass and use their own political power.

The abolition of the kapus and the discontinuation of formal religious ceremonies eroded the religious foundation of the nation and caused a vacuum to enter the social life of the Hawaiians. Historically, it is quite remarkable that while the old Hawaiian gods were being discarded, missionaries from New England were already at sea heading for the islands.

Henry 'Opukaha'ia (Obookiah)

Lured by the prospects of adventure, a number of young Hawaiians had become crew members aboard some of the ships that visited the islands. Henry 'Opukaha'ia, one of these Hawaiians, found himself in New Haven in 1809. Several years later, Obookiah (as the foreigners spelled his name) and six other Hawaiians enrolled in the Foreign Mission School at Cornwall, Conn. when it opened. It was hoped that this school would provide a number of Christian messengers who would return to their own people and spread the gospel. But Obookiah would not be among them; he died of a fever in 1817. Yet his death, and prior exemplary behavior, only encouraged the Protestant community. The American Board of Commissioners for Foreign Missions (an interdenominational body composed mostly of Presbyterians and Congregationalists) organized a mission to Hawaii in 1819.

The pioneer mission company consisted of two ordained ministers, Rev. Hiram Bingham and Rev. Asa Thurston; a physician, Dr. Thomas Holman; two teachers, Samuel Whitney and Samuel Ruggles; a printer, Elisha Loomis; a farmer, Daniel Chamberlain; plus their wives, Chamberlain's five children, and four Hawaiians who had adopted baptismal first names. Clothed in self-righteousness and armed with the sword of the "Prince of Peace," this mission company was prepared for "bloodless war" with the savage sinners whom they had to civilize and convert.

American Protestant Missionaries

Rev. Asa Thurston   Mrs. Lucy (Goodale) Thurston

Capt. Daniel Chamberlain

Departing Boston on October 23, 1819, the missionaries started their long voyage around Cape Horn and across the Pacific to Hawaii. After five months of seasickness and cramped quarters, they sighted the snow-capped peaks of Mauna Kea on the island of Hawaii on March 30, 1820. Soon after one of the young Hawaiians had returned from shore, the missionaries learned of the events that had transpired earlier: namely the death of Kamehameha the Great; the abolition of the kapus; and the destruction of the Hawaiian idols. This was convincing evidence that their God had prepared the way for them.

Several days after the missionaries met with Liholiho, the king begrudgingly allowed them to remain on the island for one year on a trial basis. After additional discussions, the king permitted them to establish another mission at Honolulu. Once settled at Honolulu, several of the missionaries accompanied a young Hawaiian named George Kaumuali'i to Waimea, Kauai where his father was king. Thinking that his son had been lost or killed, the king was overjoyed upon his son's return and he eagerly assisted the missionaries in establishing a school.

The early months were difficult for the missionaries; yet they set to work with determination and energy. But until the chiefs could be converted, the commoners and lesser chiefs would never embrace this new and strange religion. The king, for example, would have to give up four of his five wives and abstain from rum drinking in order to convert; he would forgo neither!

In October of 1821, Ka'ahumanu married King Kaumuali'i of Kauai. Shortly thereafter, she married Keali'iahonui (a son of the king), thereby increasing her hold over Kauai. Soon after her diplomatic triumph, Ka'ahumanu became ill. Nursed back to health by Sybil Bingham, she became much more receptive to Christianity. Because of Ka'ahumanu's high position, her gradual acceptance of the new religion gave it official sanction and led many chiefs into accepting this new faith.

Even before a common alphabet was adopted, the missionaries began to print spelling lessons and other materials. Now that the natives could see their own words, they could be taught to read with considerable ease. The educational work of the missionaries opened the minds and hearts of the Hawaiians to religious ideas. But they did not fully grasp the concept of Christian sin. In order to establish the western ideals of right and wrong, the missionaries had to destroy the old Hawaiian standards. Preaching endlessly about the depravation and stupidity of the Hawaiian life style, the missionaries shamed the Hawaiians into abandoning their ways and their hero ancestors.

Boki and Liliha by John Hayter

Liholiho carried on his father's policy of continuing to regard the kingdom as being under the protection of the British Empire. Desiring to see his "friend," King George IV, and get a look at the outside world, Liholiho planned a voyage to England. Perhaps fearing danger from the United States because of the large influx of American traders and missionaries, Liholiho may have wanted to obtain advice and assistance in dealing with these foreigners. Accompanied by his favorite wife (Kamāmalu), Boki (governor of Oahu) and his wife (Liliha), and a number of high-ranking chiefs plus numerous servants and interpreters, the king sailed for England on November 27, 1823 on a chartered whaler.

In Liholiho's absence, his younger brother would inherit the throne in the event of the king's death. Since this brother was only about nine years old, the position of regent was established, and Ka'ahumanu assumed this position in addition to her other duties. During the king's absence, the older chiefs chose a more orderly policy in running the affairs of government and they laid down a mini-code of laws that was based upon the teachings of the missionaries.

The royal party arrived in Portsmouth, England in mid-May of 1824. Having no advance notice of their visit, the British government hastily assigned them a guardian. Conducted to London, the royal party received new wardrobes in an attempt to make them more presentable. Their dark skin caused the Hawaiians some embarrassment in that they were ridiculed by the press and fashionable aristocrats. But generally, they received the most courteous treatment, seeing all the important buildings and places of interest, visiting theatres and occupying the royal boxes, attending receptions, etc.

Prior to meeting with King George, the royal party came down with measles. Having no immunity to the disease, their condition worsened. The attending physicians could do little, and Queen Kamāmalu died on July 8th. Grief stricken, Liholiho sank into decline and passed away on the 14th. The other Hawaiians gradually recovered, and Boki took charge. He met with King George in September, and in the discussions that followed, King George promised to protect the Hawaiian kingdom from external forces and also promised not to seize the islands. In appointing a consul to the kingdom, he recognized its independence.

Kalanimoku, Prime Minister of Hawaii
by Robert Dampier

The forty-six-gun frigate H.M.S. Blonde returned the royal party to the Hawaiian Islands. On the morning of May 11, 1825, the sumptuously decorated coffins containing the deceased king and queen were taken ashore for funeral ceremonies. After a brief service at the church, the coffins were placed inside Kalanimoku's own house until a Royal Tomb could be constructed.

On June 6, 1825, the ruling chiefs convened a national council to officially determine succession to the Hawaiian throne. In an unanimous decision, the deceased king's younger brother would become king with the title of Kamehameha III. Because the new king was only twelve years old, the council appointed Kalanimoku to be the king's special guardian and also continued the regency of Ka'ahumanu. In the meantime, he would be instructed by the missionaries in religion, reading, and writing.

CHAPTER 3

Kamehameha, III: The Constitutional Monarch

Portrait of Kamehameha III by John Mix Stanley

Portrait of Queen Kalama by John Mix Stanley

KALANI KAUIKEAOULI
BORN: August 11, 1813
FATHER: Kamehameha the Great
MOTHER: Keōpūolani, the highest-
              ranking wife of Kamehameha
RULED: June 6, 1825[1] until his
              death on December 15, 1854

KALAMA (a.k.a. HAKALELEPONI KAPAKUHAILI)
BORN: c. 1817
FATHER: Naihekukui, a minor
              Kona chief
MOTHER: I'ahu'ula
DIED: September 20, 1870

Ka'ahumanu ("The Feather Mantle") was about sixteen when she became Kamehameha the Great's wife. In full womanhood, she stood six-feet tall and grew very portly, a mark of prestige among royalty. Possessing high rank and a dictatorial temper, she ruled with a firm hand. Since many of the leading chiefs were related to her, Ka'ahumanu's edicts were seldom questioned. Her later years were filled with religious zeal, and she remained a strong friend and protector of the Protestant missionaries. This zeal and protection included a reign of terror against any natives who embraced the Catholic faith. Ka'ahumanu ruled as regent until her death on June 5, 1832.

During these years, Hawaii had become the principal replenishment port for whaling ships. By 1830, an average of more than 140 whaling ships visited the islands each year. Concentrating their visits in the spring and fall, these ships crowded the harbors at Honolulu and Lahaina. The streets filled with sailors who were intent on satisfying their long-suppressed desires for rum, gambling, and

---

[1] Ka'ahumanu served as regent during the king's minority.

Queen Ka'ahumanu by Choris

sexual fulfillment. Fights were frequent and law enforcement was lax. The Hawaiian chiefs often found themselves in the middle whenever strife arose, since the foreign population usually sided with the pleasure-bent sailors while the missionaries took the opposite, puritan stand.

Kamehameha III had grown to manhood under the influence of the missionaries and the British-American opinions favored by a majority of the foreign community. Tall, reedy, and handsome, he possessed the best physical attributes so characteristic of Hawaiian aristocracy. His shy, gentle nature and probing intellect gave little hint to the strong will hidden underneath. Like his brother before him, he enjoyed drinking, gambling, and female enticements, much to the dismay of the missionaries.

View of a Street in Honolulu[1] by J. Masselot

With Ka'ahumanu dead, the young king considered the regency ended, and he sought to rule the nation by himself. Instead, he ran into the opposition of the ruling chiefs who were reluctant to have an eighteen-year-old youth of vacillating character rule the kingdom. They insisted upon and received a joint safeguard in the form of another kuhina nui — Kīna'u, a staunch Christian. Being a daughter of

---

[1] This drawing shows Kīna'u, the kuhina nui, leaving the First Bethel Church with her maids of honor in 1837.

Kamehameha I, Kīna'u was a half sister of the young king. She also was one of the widows of Liholiho. In effect, she assumed the role of regent, and she also became governor of Oahu.

With Kīna'u running the government, Kamehameha III took to the pursuit of pleasures. The young king and his friends declared guerrilla war on Christian morality. Beginning their "war" by drinking thirty-two barrels of spirits in a week, they sought out church members and forced them to drink gin. They urged their friends to discard the Christian tabus and return to the hula, surfing, racing, and gambling of the old days. The king's example spread like a plague, emptying schools and churches. Unable to outshine the ruling chiefs, the king tried to rally his people around the symbols of their own culture.

For several years thereafter, the government was in an ambiguous state of affairs as the king vacillated between complete independence and consenting to the wishes of the older chiefs. In the beginning of 1835, the king finally conceded defeat. He reconciled with Kīna'u and left most of the responsibility for running the government in her hands.

On December 30, 1836, the king's sister (Nahi'ena'ena) died at the age of twenty. She had been struggling with an old-world love entanglement with her brother on the one hand and a new-world Christian conscience on the other. The king, chastened by her death, now turned toward the good. He gave up drinking, shut down his distilleries, and outlawed the importation of spirits. In February of 1837, Kamehameha III married Kalama in a great ceremony. Although Kalama lacked high birth, the king hoped that she would provide him with an heir. The royal couple then moved to Lahaina for about two years. The ruling chiefs appointed William Richards to be the king's instructor. Richards gradually became the king's confidential advisor, making him one of the most influential foreigners in the islands.

As the dealings with foreigners became more complex, the ruling chiefs turned to the missionaries for advice on matters of government. Initially, the missionaries refused to become directly involved. But with the ruling chiefs ignorant of world affairs, the danger always existed that some indiscreet action might prompt a major

Rev. William Richards

power to seize Hawaii. To prevent this from happening, the missionaries worked at keeping the control of the political and economic institutions in the hands of the natives.

Yet at times, Hawaii had only as much sovereignty as the major powers were willing to give her. Several times during the 1830's, the island kingdom had to knuckle under to the demands of a foreign power. One particularly harrowing confrontation took place in early July of 1839 when the French frigate *Artemise* arrived in Honolulu Harbor. Acting as a defender of Catholic missionaries in the Pacific, the French had determined that Hawaii was pursuing an anti-French policy by expelling French priests and harassing native Catholics. So the French sent Captain Laplace and his 60-gun frigate to Hawaii to teach the government respect for France and her priests. Threatening to level the city, Laplace issued a list of demands. With the threat of war looming, the government had little choice and gave in to the demands which sought to protect the personal and commercial interests of French citizens in Hawaii.

Miriam Kekāuluohi, Kuhina Nui[1]

As a new decade approached, the Protestant missionaries began to lose some of their influence over the course of events that took place in the kingdom. The actions of Captain Laplace in compelling the government to admit Catholics and French wines and brandies had successfully attacked the two policies that the missionaries considered most essential for the success of their labors. In addition, a number of the mission's staunchest supporters, including Kīna'u, died in 1839. Finally, a drastic cut in funds from New England forced the missionaries to favor self-support through investments in sugar mills or other work.

Significant changes also took place in the government regarding the relationships between the chiefs and the common people. Up to 1839, governmental power was divided into three agencies — the king, the kuhina nui, and the council of chiefs. Following the king's adoption of a policy of religious tolerance (forced on him by Captain Laplace), Kamehameha III issued a declaration of rights for his subjects. This declaration recognized the rights of all men, chiefs and commoners, and it also provided them with equal protection under the same laws.

This declaration of rights, and the constitution that followed it, were drafted with the help of a highly educated group of Hawaiians. Greatly encouraged by the

---

[1] Miriam Kekāuluohi became kuhina nui following the death of Kīna'u in April, 1839. She was the daughter of a half brother of Kamehameha the Great.

teachings of the missionaries, they favored a constitutional and representative government which would make changes favorable to the lower classes. Pressured by these educated Hawaiians, the missionaries, the foreign community, and foreign commanders of warships, the king gave his subjects a new constitution. Signed into law on October 8, 1840, the constitution restated the existing political institutions and laws that were in effect and, more importantly, called for the creation of a "representative body" chosen by the people to become a part of the legislature. For the first time, the common people had a share in the political power of the government.

Events having international ramifications began to unfold in the early 1840's. The United States Exploring Expedition arrived in the fall of 1840 and spent about six months in the islands. In this same year, Great Britain annexed New Zealand, and France had several warships in the South Pacific. With its future security in question, the government of Hawaii began an attempt to have its independence recognized by these nations.

Lord George Paulet

In mid-1842, the French seized the Marquesas Islands, and several months later, France established a protectorate in Tahiti. While many people were wondering whether Hawaii might be next, the commander of the British squadron in the Pacific, Rear Admiral Richard Thomas, ordered the frigate *Carysfort* to proceed to the Hawaiian and Society Islands to investigate the alleged mistreatment of British subjects. The frigate, commanded by Lord George Paulet, arrived in Honolulu on February 10, 1843.

The king, being in Lahaina as usual, had to be sent for before any action could be taken. He arrived a week later, declined a private audience with Paulet, and offered instead to receive written communications through Dr. Gerrit P. Judd, his confidential agent. In turn, Paulet refused to deal with Judd and sent the king a lengthy list of demands which required compliance by the following afternoon.

The following morning, foreign residents were notified of an expected attack on the city. An English brig offered asylum to British residents. The normally quiet streets turned into an unusual spectacle as the foreign residents crowded the streets, pushing and pulling carts filled with personal belongings as they made their way to safety. After lengthy discussions with his advisors, the king yielded under protest, fearing that the British would use this episode as an excuse to seize the islands.

Interior of Honolulu's Fort

During a series of daily conferences held between February 20th through the 23rd, the king and Dr. Judd concluded that the British were determined to seize Hawaii. With cession inevitable, the decision had to be made: cession to France and the United States; or cession to Great Britain. Dr. Judd favored cession to Great Britain, and the king and the ruling chiefs agreed. Although they considered Paulet their enemy, they considered England their "FRIEND." On February 25, 1843, the formal ceremony of a provisional cession to Great Britain took place within the fort. The king gave a short speech which Dr. Judd translated. "I have given away the life of the land," the king declared, but he went on to state that the government would take every possible step to restore Hawaii's independence. After the king's speech, the deed of cession was read. Then the Hawaiian flag was replaced by the British flag as the fort and the British frigate exchanged a twenty-one-gun salute.

The islands were under British rule for about five months. On July 26, Rear Admiral Thomas arrived in Honolulu aboard his flagship. He had immediately sailed from Valparaiso (Chile) as soon as he had heard of Paulet's actions. During several days of conferences between Admiral Thomas, the king, and Dr. Judd, it became apparent that the admiral intended to restore Hawaii's independence, subject to securing certain agreements from the king. These agreements, somewhat in the form of a treaty, closely guarded the rights and privileges of British subjects in Hawaii and guaranteed them equality with the most-favored foreigners. Since these articles were subject to whatever arrangements would be made in London, the king signed them, relying on the good faith and friendly intentions of the admiral.

Rear Admiral Richard Thomas

At formal ceremonies held on the morning of July 31, the Hawaiian flag was again raised over the tiny kingdom. The roar and reverberations of cannon fire from the English and American ships plus responding volleys from the fort and Punch Bowl battery announced Hawaii's independence. Later in the afternoon, a thanksgiving service was held at Kawaiaha'o Church in which the king was said to have proclaimed the words: "Ua mau ke ea o ka 'āina i ka pono." ("The life of the land is perpetuated in righteousness.") Ten days of festivities and rejoicing followed.

Although Admiral Thomas had acted upon his own initiative in restoring Hawaii's independence, his actions were based on his knowledge of British policy and he was confident that they would be approved (as they later were). By the end of November, Great Britain and France had signed a joint declaration which recognized Hawaii's independence. Although the three great powers had now recognized the independence of the islands, treaty relations were still not on an equitable basis. The United States didn't make a treaty; France still considered the Laplace Treaty of 1839 in effect; and Great Britain drafted a new treaty without consulting the Hawaiian government — it merely sent the document to the islands for signature.

Now Hawaii began to alter its course of action so as to strengthen itself and give itself dignity. Ironically, to achieve these new ambitions, the government had to appoint a number of foreigners to positions of responsibility. The king's advisors withdrew the king from the easy-going, social relations that he had previously maintained with foreigners, and surrounded the throne with pomp and royal etiquette. Hoping to make the king's administration more respectable, the government adopted the rules of precedence and etiquette which the great powers had adopted at the Congress of Vienna in 1815.

Lacking the knowledge and experience to deal with the growing complexity of governmental affairs, the native chiefs were mostly excluded from the new positions that were being created in an attempt to catch up with western civilization. Dr. Gerrit P. Judd gradually rose in status to become the most conspicuous and influential member of the government. Keenly aware of the kingdom's weakness in matters of physical force (it lacked both a standing army and navy), Judd sought to maintain the sovereignty of the nation through his own high moral power. Another influential foreigner was Robert Crichton Wyllie, a Scotsman. Wyllie became minister of foreign relations in March of 1845 after being recommended by Judd. Despite becoming alienated from Judd several years later, Wyllie continued in his post until he died on October 19, 1865.

Prior to 1844, the legislature met in Lahaina. No session was held in 1844. After that date, the sessions were held in Honolulu, and the laws became more elaborate and precise in their phraseology. A significant action undertaken by the legislature at this time was the creation of a land commission which revolutionized the landholding system. The commission decided that vested interests in the land belonged to the government (the king), the landlord, and the tenant. While the legislature defined the rights of these groups and provided procedures by which tenants might acquire land, no solution for dividing the land between the king and the landlords was reached for nearly two years. Finally in December of 1847, a plan was adopted which cleared the way for the "Great Māhele." Shortly after the final division was made with the last chief, the king divided his lands into two parts: the smaller part became "Crown Lands"[1] which were his own private lands; the other, larger part became government lands, set apart forever for the chiefs and the people.

Although the common people had not been forgotten, no specific fraction of

---

[1] Eventually, "Crown Lands" referred to the lands attached to the crown itself and not the wearer of the crown. They became distinct from government lands and from private lands that the ruling monarch owned as an individual.

the lands had been set aside for them in the general settlement. While businessmen, missionaries, heirs of deceased foreigners, and the humblest of men came forward to present their claims to the land commission, few native Hawaiians made any claims. So the missionaries and some foreigners started a movement to improve the condition of the natives by giving them land in fee simple and then freeing them from the labor tax.

Kamehameha III (About 1850)

In 1850, all native tenants were granted "kuleanas" (fee-simple titles) to the lands occupied and cultivated by them, except for houselots in Honolulu, Hilo, and Lahaina. The only condition attached to the kuleana was that the tenant had to present a claim to the land commission. Additional government lands were sold at $0.50 an acre to natives who had not received sufficient lands. The government thus wiped away the last remnants of the old feudal land system. A great buying and selling frenzy followed in the years ahead. Yet while many foreigners bought land, many natives sold their lands. They didn't fully understand the sudden liberty thrust upon them. But they did understand the freedom to sell their land, and sell they did! During the ensuing fifty years, foreigners would own four times the amount of land held by the natives and chiefs combined.

Inspired by American expansion in the west, annexation rumors abounded. Growing trade with China and the prospects of trading with Japan increased the importance of Hawaii to the United States. In addition, the strategic value of Pearl Harbor had been recognized. The population of the islands kept changing in favor of foreigners and part-Hawaiians as the pure native population kept decreasing. The agricultural development of the islands, tied closely to the West Coast for its market, produced a small but influential group of businessmen whose sentiment for annexation grew out of their desires for a duty-free market.

The annexation movement in Honolulu was interrupted by a smallpox epidemic which broke out in May of 1853. But by the beginning of 1854, the United States and Hawaii continued the talks. On December 15, 1854, Kamehameha III died. Although he had been in poor health for a year or more, the illness that ended his life lasted less than a week. With him died any hopes for annexation. Since the king had no surviving children, he had adopted Alexander Liholiho as his son and had proclaimed him heir to the throne in April of 1853. Possessing a brilliant mind, ambitious, and concerned for his country's independence, the twenty-year-old prince held great influence with the king. Having been exposed to color prejudice in the United States, Prince Alexander was staunchly anti-American and he used numerous delaying tactics to stall negotiations. One of the new king's first official acts was to terminate the annexation negotiations.

CHAPTER 4

Kamehameha, IV:
The Aristocratic King

Kamehameha IV in 1855

Queen Emma

ALEXANDER LIHOLIHO

BORN: February 9, 1834
FATHER: Mataio Kekūanaō'a,
governor of Oahu
(1839 - 1868)
MOTHER: Kīna'u, daughter of
Kamehameha I; kuhina nui
and governor of Oahu
(1832 - 1839)
RULED: Jan. 11, 1855 until his
death on Nov. 30, 1863

EMMA NĀEA ROOKE

BORN: January 2, 1836
FATHER: George Nāea, a chief
MOTHER: Fanny Kekelaokalani
Young
ADOPTED: by her maternal aunt,
Grace Kama'iku'i Young
and her husband, Dr.
Thomas C. B. Rooke
DIED: April 25, 1885

The funeral for Kamehameha III, last son of Kamehameha the Great, was held on January 10, 1855 with pomp and pageantry, tears and chants befitting the noblest of Hawaiian kings. On the following day, Alexander Liholiho, the adopted son of the former king, took the oath of office in his formal inauguration as Kamehameha IV. During the ceremony, held before an immense crowd of both natives and foreigners in Kawaiaha'o Church, the new king gave his coronation address first in Hawaiian and then in English. He swore to uphold the constitution and increase civilization and its good virtues, and he sought to preserve the independence of his kingdom. His nearly three years of serving as a member of the Privy Council had provided Liholiho with valuable political experience, and he stood ready to accept the serious responsibilities of his high position.

Dr. Gerrit P. Judd with Prince Lot Kamehameha (left) and Prince Alexander Liholiho (right) in Paris, 1850

At the age of fifteen, Liholiho and his brother, Prince Lot, had accompanied Dr. Gerrit P. Judd on a diplomatic mission to France. Their journey, which occurred in 1849 and 1850, also included stops in England and the United States. This trip had instilled in Liholiho a great admiration for English institutions, and his ideas and tastes became more European than Hawaiian. In this regard, Kamehameha IV firmly believed in the aristocracy's right and duty to rule over the lower classes. While in the United States, Prince Alexander had experienced color prejudice when he was mistaken for a servant by a train conductor and ordered to leave the compartment. While the mistake was quickly corrected, it nevertheless left the young prince with a lasting bitterness toward anything American.

John Young II (Keoni Ana)

The new king's cabinet remained essentially the same as the previous cabinet since Liholiho reappointed all the previous ministers. While John Young II continued as minister of the interior, his position as kuhina nui was not renewed. Instead, the king appointed his sister, Princess Victoria Kamāmalu, to this position.

Prince Lot was appointed a general to command the armed forces, and he also became an important member of the government, taking part in deliberations of the cabinet, the Privy Council, and the House of Nobles.

Kamehameha IV had ascended the throne as a bachelor, one month short of turning twenty-one. Shortly after coming to power, the king's faithful advisor, Robert Wyllie, encouraged the king to marry in order to give stability to the crown and to continue the monarchy under a native dynasty. Liholiho concurred, and he decided to marry his childhood sweetheart, Emma Nāea Rooke. Emma was the granddaughter of John Young and a great-grandniece of Kamehameha the Great. Educated at the Royal School, Emma spoke fluent English. She had received a refined upbringing, and her natural gifts of amiability and cordiality made her well liked.

Albert Edward Kauikeaouli, The Prince of Hawaii

The royal wedding took place in Kawaiaha'o Church on June 19, 1856, and it was one of the grandest affairs to take place in the kingdom up to that date. The gala event inspired a number of social functions during the ensuing months, including a grand ball hosted by the Chinese merchants of Honolulu. Less than two years later, a royal prince was born on May 20, 1858, rekindling the hopes of the Hawaiian race. With the consent of the Privy Council, the little prince received the title of "His Royal Highness the Prince of Hawaii," and he was formally christened Albert Edward Kauikeaouli Leiopapa a Kamehameha. The young prince became an instant and intimate part of the royal couple's private life, and he was taken nearly everywhere they went.

During the reign of Kamehameha IV, Honolulu continued to expand and prosper. In 1850, the population of Honolulu numbered about 10,000, and nearly twenty percent of the city's residents were foreigners. The 1853 census showed a total population for the Hawaiian Islands of 73,138, a decrease of over 35,000 from the census of 1835. As each year passed, Honolulu took on a greater resemblance to a New England seaport. Many new residences and businesses were constructed of stone or lumber imported from the Pacific Northwest. Warehouses, a shipyard, a courthouse, a market building for trading produce, plus hotels, billiard saloons, and countless other business and government buildings lined the streets as the city expanded. Imposing residences of chiefs, foreign consuls, government officials, sea captains, businessmen, and missionaries dotted the beautiful Nu'uanu Valley just north of the city.

Whaling Off the Coast of Hawaii

Whaling continued to dominate the economy in the decade of the 1850's even though fears were being raised about the eventual withdrawal of the whaling fleet. These fears were well founded, based on several poor years and temporary shrinkages in the size of the whaling fleet. But overall, whaling continued at high levels. The period between 1843 and 1860 has often been called the "golden age" of whaling in Hawaii's history. Three peak years stood out: 1846, 1853, and 1859. The islands were so dependent on the whaling fleet that the government encouraged their visits and gave them preferential treatment in terms of harbor and transit dues. Nearly every form of business enterprise in the cities depended in one way or another on the semiannual visits of the whaling fleet. The government also benefited directly through the collection of various harbor fees and the imposition of fines by the police courts. Native policemen, paid a percentage of the fines, eagerly enforced the laws against disturbing the peace, drunkenness, "furious riding," etc.

Fortunately for the Hawaiian economy, the decline of whaling occurred gradually. (It came to an end in 1880). This slow decline enabled businessmen to seek alternate opportunities. The sugar industry, in particular, progressively replaced the whaling industry as Hawaii's main source of income. An expansion of merchant shipping to and from the islands also took place at this time. The development and settlement of California and the Oregon Territory, the American Civil War, and the introduction of transcontinental rail service all had a compounding effect in shifting much of Hawaii's trade from Atlantic to Pacific ports. Gradually, the port of San Francisco surpassed all the rest.

While the king and queen frequently presented operas and musicals to aristocratic audiences, they never forgot the plight of the common Hawaiian people and the decimation of their numbers by disease. In an attempt to help his subjects, the king pressed hard for the establishment of a state hospital. To achieve this goal, the king and queen personally solicited donations and pledges from their friends to finance the hospital. Construction of Queen's Hospital, named in honor of Queen Emma, began in 1859. Expanded and modernized numerous times, it still serves the community on the same site in downtown Honolulu.

Two other events that took place in 1859 had a profound influence on the establishment of the Episcopal Church in Hawaii. The first event was the serious illness of Robert Wyllie, minister of foreign relations. Wyllie's long ordeal renewed his interests in religion, and he longed to establish an Episcopal chapel in Honolulu. The second event involved the king and his private secretary, a young American named Henry A. Neilson. In August, the king and queen and a large royal party left Honolulu for a holiday on the islands of Hawaii and Maui. While on Maui (or perhaps even earlier), the king heard malicious gossip that his secretary was having an affair with the queen. Brooding over the matter, King Alexander spent several days at sea, drinking heavily and deliberating his course of action. On the evening of September 11, he came ashore and sought out Neilson. Without uttering a sound, the king walked up to Neilson and shot him in the chest at close range. Miraculously the wound, though serious, was not fatal.

Neilson lived for two and a half years, although the wound undoubtedly contributed to his early death. The king's position shielded him from any prosecution, and no legal notice was ever taken of the incident. Nevertheless, the king was filled with remorse, and later inquiries into the affair proved his suspicions to be groundless. Strengthened by Wyllie and Queen Emma, the king set the wheels in motion to establish an Episcopal Church in Hawaii. Now he firmly believed that their doctrines and rituals were more compatible with his monarchy.

The Reverend Thomas Nettleship Staley was designated as bishop to head the new missionary diocese in Hawaii. The bishop and his family left London on August 17, 1862. The Hawaiian royal couple eagerly awaited the bishop's arrival because they intended that his first official act would be the baptism of their young son, the Prince of Hawaii. Queen Victoria of England had agreed to be the child's godmother by proxy, and she had ordered a costly silver christening cup for her distant godson.

Queen Emma[1]

The silver cup arrived ahead of Bishop Staley in the care of the new British consul general to Hawaii, William W.F. Synge and his wife. Mrs. Synge had been designated by Queen Victoria to act as her proxy at the baptism. Their ship arrived on August 22, 1862. The following morning, before landing, Synge received word

---

[1] Queen Emma is standing next to the christening cup (a silver vase) that was a gift from Queen Victoria of England.

that the Prince of Hawaii had come down with a mysterious disease. Some called it "brain fever;"[1] in any event, the attending physicians could do nothing. The Reverend E. W. Clark of Kawaiaha'o Church performed a hurried baptism according to the rites of the Church of England. The little prince clung to life for several days in a hopeless state. He succumbed to his disease on August 27 at the tender age of four, leaving his parents and the Hawaiian community in a state of intense sorrow and desolation.

Yet despite the support of the monarchy, the Hawaiian Reformed Catholic Church (as it was initially called) failed to achieve the great success that its founders had hoped for. It met stiff competition from the Protestant and Catholic Churches which were already well established in Hawaii. In addition to the wide differences in ideology and forms of worship, the new church was plagued by internal dissension and handicapped by inadequate monetary support. Bishop Staley, who had arrived in Hawaii in October of 1862, resigned in 1870, and the name of the church was later changed to the Anglican Church in Hawaii.

Kamehameha IV in Later Life

Following the death of his young son, Kamehameha IV kept himself out of the public eye as much as possible. Grief over the death of his son, guilt over the shooting and later death of his private secretary, and chronic asthma all began to take their toll on the king. He became bad-tempered and moody; he ate less and drank more; and his asthmatic attacks increased both in frequency and severity to the point where he could scarcely breathe. The final attack came on the morning of November 30, 1863 with Queen Emma at his side desperately trying to breathe life into her choking and dying husband. Her valiant efforts failed, and the young king joined his royal ancestors.

The sudden, unexpected death of Kamehameha IV left the kingdom without any formal successor since the royal couple had no living children. In the absence of a direct heir, the king's brother was considered to be the lawful successor to the throne. During the afternoon of November 30, a document was drawn up by the kuhina nui and approved by the Privy Council which proclaimed Prince Lot as king of the Hawaiian Islands with the title and style of Kamehameha V.

---

[1] In attempting to cool off his son from an uncontrollable fit of passion, the king held his son's head under a spout of cold, running water. Whether or not this cold-water immersion had anything to do with the resulting disease is unclear. But in any event, the king blamed himself for his son's death. (Prince Albert was the last child born to a reigning Hawaiian monarch.)

Hulihe'e Palace, Kailua-Kona, Hawaii
Daughters of Hawaii Collection

The Kuakini Room at Hulihe'e Palace
Daughters of Hawaii Collection

King Kalākaua

(b.) November 16, 1836 – January 20, 1891 (d.)

Queen Kapiʻolani's
Crown

Queen Kapiʻolani

(b.) December 31, 1834 – June 24, 1899 (d.)

The Queen Emma Summer Palace
Photo by Author

The Edinburgh Room of the Queen Emma Summer Palace
Daughters of Hawaii Collection

CHAPTER 5

Kamehameha, V: The Last Kamehameha

Kamehameha V in Military Uniform

LOT KAMEHAMEHA
("THE BACHELOR KING")

BORN: December 11, 1830
FATHER: Mataio Kekūanaō'a,
           governor of Oahu
           (1839 - 1868)
MOTHER: Kīna'u, daughter of
           Kamehameha I; kuhina nui
           and governor of Oahu
           (1832 - 1839)
RULED: November 30, 1863 until
           his death on
           December 11, 1872

Lot Kamehameha, in assuming his role as king of the Hawaiian Islands, refused to be publicly inaugurated and likewise refused to take the oath to maintain the Constitution of 1852. He believed that Hawaii's sovereigns had the right to change the constitution at will since it had been a grant from Kamehameha III. While Lot's political ideas were very similar to those of his deceased brother, there were marked differences between the two men. Kamehameha IV had been well proportioned and elegant in appearance. He displayed high culture and social graces, and many of his court functions were patterned after those of the British. Lot, being large and heavy, resembled the founder of the dynasty, and he was more Hawaiian in his point of view. Although both brothers had been educated at the Royal School and had traveled extensively, Lot cast aside the snobbery and gentlemanly manners of his predecessor, preferring instead many of the old customs. He dressed modestly and often rode around Honolulu alone on his old horse. Yet he was greatly respected by the people. Strong-willed and unexcitable, Lot appeared to possess great energy, perseverance, and strength of will.

Shortly after ascending the throne, Kamehameha V assembled his cabinet, gathering around him trusted men who would serve the autocratic new king throughout most of his reign. Robert Wyllie continued to serve as minister of foreign relations, and he advised the king on making the other appointments. The king's father, Mataio Kekūanaō'a, assumed the position of kuhina nui, replacing the king's sister (Princess Victoria Kamāmalu).

One of the early proclamations issued by Kamehameha V called for publicly elected delegates of the people to meet with the king and the nobles in a consti-

Robert Crichton Wyllie

tutional convention scheduled to begin on July 7, 1864. It was the king's desire to propose a new constitution more favorable to the crown rather than to propose new amendments to the old constitution. The convention started as scheduled, but during August it deadlocked over voter qualifications. The king took the initiative and abruptly dismissed the convention. He then abrogated the Constitution of 1852 and soon thereafter gave the people his own constitution.

Mataio Kekūanaō'a

On August 20, 1864, Kamehameha V signed his new constitution into law and also took an oath to maintain it. Although this new constitution was based upon the draft previously submitted to the convention, it contained a number of modifications and changes. The significant changes abolished the office of kuhina nui, greatly curtailed the powers of the Privy Council, increased the powers and privileges of the king, and strengthened the administrative powers of the king's cabinet. In effect, it greatly restored the power of the monarchy.

The king's appointment of a Frenchman to his cabinet convinced many Americans living in Hawaii that Lot had adopted an anti-American policy. Actually, the king's foreign policy remained much the same as it had been under the previous reign of his brother. Basically, its prime objective continued to be the safeguarding of the kingdom's independence. Yet feelings of mistrust between Americans, Frenchmen, and Englishmen living in the islands continued to grow and were strengthened by France's and Great Britain's unfriendly stance toward the United States during the Civil War.

Following the Civil War, the United States Navy assigned the *USS Lackawanna* to the islands for an indefinite stay. She arrived in Honolulu on February 9, 1867. In addition to strengthening America's position in the islands, the *Lackawanna* was also under orders to protect American interests. Undoubtedly, the presence of an American warship would also have a calming effect should a serious political crisis develop.

The growth of steamship travel between Hawaii and the West Coast of the United States, Australia, and New Zealand caused a large increase in the number of visitors to the islands. These visitors included Mark Twain who came to Hawaii in March of 1866 as a correspondent for the Sacramento Union. Intending to stay only one month, Twain (traveling under his real name — Samuel Clemens) stayed four months, and in the process, wrote twenty-five letters to the Union describing with caustic humor and wit his experiences in Hawaii and his impressions of her people. Another famous visitor of that time was Alfred Ernest Albert, the Duke of Edinburgh, who came to Hawaii on a state visit in 1869.

The Hawaiian Hotel

The arrival and departure of Twain, the Duke of Edinburgh, and others including envoys, politicians, merchants, and opportunists created the need for hotel accommodations to lodge similar visitors in the future. Since no private individuals were willing or capable of undertaking such an enterprise, the king felt that the government should undertake such a project. Construction began in May of 1871, and the Hawaiian Hotel, located on the corner of Hotel and Richards streets, formally opened with a subscription ball on February 29, 1872.[1]

The Hawaiian Hotel was only one of a number of ambitious building programs initiated by Kamehameha V in an effort to present a credible and pleasing face to the governments of the world whose representatives continually visited his kingdom. Another major undertaking was the construction of Ali'iōlani Hale ("House of the Chief Unto Heaven"). This project was supposed to be a new palace, but it met with numerous delays and financial problems. So its initial purpose was dropped, and it became a government office building when it was completed in 1874.

Buildings of lesser scope included 'Iolani Barracks (to house the Royal Household Guards), a new prison, the Royal Mausoleum, new schoolhouses and ware-

---

[1] Private individuals "subscribed" to Hotel Bonds and then received a proportion of the rents in lieu of interest. In the course of time, the name of the hotel was changed to the Royal Hawaiian Hotel, and it passed into private hands. During World War I, it was converted into the present Armed Forces YMCA.

Ali'iōlani Hale (Government Office Building)

houses, an insane asylum, a quarantine building (to process the flood of immigrants brought to Hawaii by the sugar planters), and other government structures. These heavy expenditures put a severe strain on the financial resources of the tiny kingdom. Since all these projects could not be financed from general revenues, the government resorted to borrowing with great difficulty and at high interest rates (12% on most loans and up to 18% on others). As a result of this excessive borrowing, Hawaii's national debt stood at over $350,000 on March 31, 1874!

Since Kamehameha V preferred to remain a bachelor, many of his ministers worried about a successor. In 1864, Lot proclaimed his sister, Princess Victoria Kamāmalu as heir presumptive. But she died on May 26, 1866, again raising the question of succession. The king's ministers frequently proposed marriage to various eligible female ali'is, including Queen Emma (the king's sister-in-law), fearing that the uncertainty of succession played into the hands of those factions who favored annexation to the United States. While the king was in love with his deceased brother's wife, there seemed to be too many obstacles in the way, including religious objections and Emma's devotion to the memory of her deceased husband.

Lot Kamehameha in His Later Years

Throughout the remainder of his reign, Lot remained stubborn and refused to name a successor. In his later years, he became even more obese, and his heavy frame made it difficult for him to move about. In time, he could no longer ride a horse, and thereafter, he spent most of his time indoors. Abandoning physical activity, Lot soon took to his bed. He steadily grew weaker, and on December 11, 1872, a final effort was put forth to have the king appoint a successor. Reluctantly, he named High Chiefess Bernice Pauahi Bishop. But she refused, suggesting instead the king's half sister, Ruth Ke'elikolani, and then Queen Emma. However the king passed on these suggestions, and before the matter could be discussed again, Lot Kamehameha died while preparations were under way for his birthday celebration. Thus the Kamehameha dynasty came to an abrupt end.

CHAPTER 6

William C. Lunalilo: The People's King

WILLIAM C. LUNALILO

BORN: January 31, 1835

FATHER: Charles Kana'ina, a minor chief and friend of the Kamehamehas

MOTHER: Miriam Kekāuluohi, one of the five wives of Kamehameha the Great and, after his death, one of the wives of his son, Kamehameha II; married Charles Kana'ina in 1834; kuhina nui (1839–1845)

RULED: January 8, 1873 until his death on February 3, 1874

William C. Lunalilo

David Kalākaua

Ruth Ke'elikolani

Bernice Pauahi Bishop

Contenders for the Throne

The death of Kamehameha V threw the Hawaiian nation into a monarchial crisis. Since the dead king had refused to name a successor, this decision passed to the legislature under the provisions of the Constitution of 1864. The king's cabinet promptly scheduled a meeting of the legislature for January 8, 1873. Four ali'i soon stood out as possible candidates for the throne. They were William Charles Lunalilo, Ruth Ke'elikolani, David Kalākaua, and Bernice Pauahi.

William Lunalilo, a cousin of the deceased king, had the best natural claim to the throne since he was a grandson of a half brother of Kamehameha the Great. But because of Lunalilo's political naivete, frivolity, and excessive drinking habits, Lot Kamehameha had considered him a "fool" and had refused to name him as a successor. Perhaps too, Lot was jealous of Lunalilo's immense popularity with the people. Ruth Ke'elikolani, a half sister of the deceased king, was the favorite candidate among many of the chiefs because of her strict adherence to the "old" Hawaiian ways. Being six-feet tall and weighing over four hundred pounds, Ruth ruled as governess of the island of Hawaii. But her genealogy was much too controversial, and few people considered her a suitable candidate for the position of ruling monarch.

David Kalākaua's blood line came from the fierce and independent chiefs of Kona who had supported Kamehameha the Great in his successful quest of uniting all the islands under one ruler. Well-educated, fluent in English, and possessing polished manners, Kalākaua mingled freely in the general society. His long years in the Hawaiian legislature had sharpened his political skills, making him a good contender for the throne. Bernice Pauahi, a great grand-daughter of Kamehameha the Great, remained in the running because the late king had specifically designated her prior to his death. But she remained steadfast in her refusal to accept the throne.

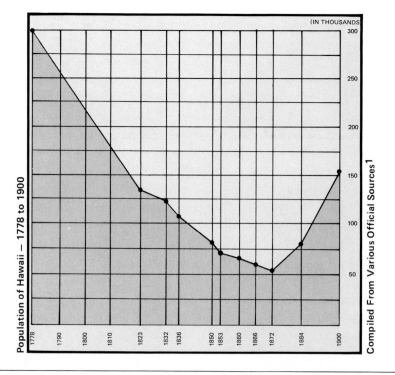

1 Two of these sources are "Demographic Statistics of Hawaii, 1778-1965" by Robert C. Schmitt and "Atlas of Hawaii," by the University of Hawaii, Dept. of Geography. See the bibliography at the end of this book for publication data.

The overwhelming popular support for Lunalilo soon brought the number of candidates down to two: Lunalilo and Kalākaua. Resisting the demands of many of his enthusiastic supporters that he go to the palace and proclaim himself king, Lunalilo instead issued a manifesto on December 16 in which he proclaimed himself as the rightful heir to the throne. He offered to submit his claim to a vote by the people in a special election. Pledging only to restore the Constitution of 1852, Lunalilo sought a peaceful and legal path to the throne. On December 28, Kalākaua issued his platform in anticipation of the upcoming election.

On January 1, 1873, a large number of male subjects in the kingdom went to the polls and voted almost unanimously for Lunalilo. Meeting several days later, the legislature cast its own ballots, and Lunalilo emerged as the unanimous choice. On the following day, January 9, Lunalilo went to Kawaiaha'o Church and made two short speeches: one to the legislature and the other to the general populace. In this latter speech, the new king appealed to all Hawaiians to make every effort to reverse the continuing decline in the native population.

While Lunalilo possessed a superior intelligence and was well read in English literature, he had little experience in practical matters. This handsome, fun-loving and spoiled prince had literally no experience in financial affairs since his guardians had seen to his personal affairs for many years. Despite having been a member of the Privy Council and the House of Nobles, Lunalilo had acquired almost no experience in public administration. Well aware of his weaknesses, the new king quickly put together a cabinet that consisted of men of high character and ability who would add strength to his new government. With the exception of a Scotsman, all the new cabinet ministers were Americans. The king then sent a message to the legislature recommending a number of amendments that would nullify numerous changes made in the Constitution of 1864 if they were enacted. Unlike his predecessor, Lunalilo sought a more democratic approach to changing the constitution.

Several weeks after Lunalilo ascended the throne, customhouse figures were released showing that the quantity of sugar exported had fallen off by nearly five million pounds. In addition to the smaller crop, the average price that the sugar planters received was lower than it had been for many years. The depressed state of the sugar industry naturally spilled over into other segments of the business community, and once again the old solutions of reciprocity and annexation began making the rounds in private as well as public conversations.

The reforms that the new king so vigorously launched early in his reign were slow to materialize, and the change in kings did little to erase the problems that plagued the tiny island kingdom. American warships and military men visited the islands to check on the strategic importance of Pearl Harbor, a lease on which was being touted as a way of obtaining a reciprocity treaty with the United States. Leprosy, although only mildly contagious, continued to spread among the natives. The new government responded with an immediate and energetic effort to fully enforce the segregationist and isolationist plans that were adopted earlier. Before the year ended, over five hundred new victims of the disease were discovered and sent to the leper settlement on Molokai. Friends and relatives of the afflicted were no longer allowed to visit the settlement. This policy reversal caused bitter resentment among the Hawaiian people toward their government and also toward the king, since he approved of the policy.

While Lunalilo escaped Leprosy, he experienced chest pains and came down with a severe cold in the middle of August, 1873. Avoiding public contact, Lunalilo retreated to his summer palace at Waikiki with his ministers, physicians, and close friends. While his health soon improved, he never returned to a normal state of health. The king's doctors called for complete abstention from intoxicating drinks, but Lunalilo would not hear of it. Recovering from pneumonia, he contracted pulmonary tuberculosis in his weakened condition.

In September, the sick and weary monarch faced a mutiny by the Household Troops who rebelled against their officers. After several days, the king finally agreed to protect the mutineers from injury and then he abruptly disbanded the Household Troops except for the Royal Band. This action left the kingdom without any regular, organized military protection. With the government humiliated, Lunalilo tried to sidetrack the crisis by returning to the palace in Honolulu. In November, the king's health began to deteriorate again, and the king attempted to recuperate in the warmer sunshine and clear sea air at Kailua on the island of Hawaii. But this change didn't help and the king's condition grew steadily worse. In mid-January of 1874, Lunalilo returned to Honolulu as an invalid, having had to be carried ashore.

Last Photograph of King Lunalilo

Lunalilo clung to life for about two more weeks before dying on February 3, 1874, barely passing his thirty-ninth birthday. His reign was the shortest of any monarch — one year and twenty-five days. Often called the "people's king," Lunalilo left all of his estate for the establishment of a home for "poor, destitute and infirm people of Hawaiian blood or extraction, giving preference to old people." The Lunalilo Home later became an enduring monument to his memory.

Like his predecessor Kamehameha V, Lunalilo died a bachelor and consequently had no direct heirs to the throne. Likewise, he failed to appoint a successor, saying repeatedly that he had not made up his mind. Having felt slighted by the clannish Kamehameha family, Lunalilo's last wish was to be buried away from them. So instead of being entombed in the Royal Mausoleum, Lunalilo was buried in a separate mausoleum that was constructed after his death. (See chapter 10 for additional information on royal burial sites.)

CHAPTER 7

David Kalākaua: The Merry Monarch

Kalākaua in Uniform

Queen Kapi'olani

DAVID LA'AMEA KALĀKAUA
BORN: November 16, 1836
FATHER: Caesar Kapa'akea, son of
Kamanawa II — grand nephew
of Kamanawa I of Kona who
supported Kamehameha I
MOTHER: Keohokalole
RULED: February 12, 1874 until his
death on January 20, 1891

JULIA KAPI'OLANI
BORN: December 31, 1834
FATHER: Kūhiō, high chief of Hilo
MOTHER: Princess Kinoiki, a daughter
of Kaumuali'i (last king
of Kauai)
DIED: June 24, 1899

Once again, the Hawaiian Kingdom was thrown into disarray over the matter of succession, and the names of the same ali'is came up for consideration to replace the deceased king. But of this group, only three were considered serious contenders: Queen Emma, Bernice Pauahi, and David Kalākaua who became the most active contender. Having accepted his earlier defeat with dignity, Kalākaua received an appointment as a colonel on Lunalilo's military staff.

Queen Emma, who had previously supported Lunalilo, announced her candidacy and asserted that the late king had intended for her to become his successor. Since most of the local newspapers supported Kalākaua, Queen Emma and her followers resorted to distributing placards and handbills throughout the city, thereby initiating a propaganda war. Bernice Pauahi, handicapped by an American husband, displayed little desire in seeking the throne.

While a number of Americans in Honolulu distrusted Kalākaua, they perceived Queen Emma as being pro-British. So these Americans gave their support to Kalākaua. The king's cabinet scheduled a special legislative meeting for February 12 to take up the matter of succession. This gave the two candidates sufficient time to wage a furious campaign for the vacant throne. With three warships in Honolulu Harbor (two American and one British), the American Minister, Henry A. Peirce, arranged a shore-to-ship signal with the senior American naval officer to land troops should violence erupt.

When the legislative ballots were counted, Kalākaua emerged victorious. As a committee left the courthouse to notify him, its members were attacked by Queen Emma's supporters who had just heard the results. In a wild melee that followed, the angry supporters demolished a carriage and used the pieces as clubs. They stormed the courthouse, ravaged its interior, and attacked the legislators who were desperately trying to escape.

The police were totally ineffective in controlling the riot, and since there was no standing army, the new government asked the American minister for help. Peirce sent his prearranged signal, and 150 armed marines and bluejackets came ashore. Shortly thereafter, about 70 British troops joined the Americans in dispersing the crowd and restoring order. The troops remained ashore for about eight days until tensions eased.

On the 13th, Kalākaua took the oath of office inside the riot-torn courthouse. The diplomatic representatives of the United States, Great Britain, and France promptly recognized Kalākaua as the new sovereign, and later the same day, Queen Emma did likewise. She also asked her supporters to accept the new king and avoid any further acts of violence.

Kalākaua appointed his younger brother, Prince William Pitt Leleiohoku, as his successor, thereby restoring to the crown the function of selecting kings. Next, he appointed his cabinet, recognizing the cosmopolitan nature of the community. Later, he created a new military organization which consisted of one regular company known as the "Royal Guards" and three volunteer companies. Kalākaua had a special fondness for military matters, and he took great pride in wearing elaborate military uniforms.

Since 1863, Kalākaua had been married to Julia Kapi'olani, the widow of Benjamin Namakeha. But despite their many years of marriage, they had no children. The new queen accompanied her husband on a royal procession through the kingdom, and everywhere they went, they received enthusiastic welcomes. In speaking to the people, Kalākaua projected a fatherly image and always dwelt on the decline of the Hawaiian race. He hoped to restore new life and new vigor into the nation.

The sugar planters and other business interests lost no time in trying to revive reciprocity negotiations with the United States. While Kalākaua didn't oppose the treaty, he did oppose surrendering Hawaiian territory to obtain one. In order to get the stalled negotiations going again, Kalākaua decided to visit the United States in November. After sailing to San Francisco, the king and his royal party traveled by train to Washington where they arrived on December 12. For ten days, Kalākaua was treated to an almost continuous round of entertainment which was highlighted by a state dinner with President Grant. While the king didn't participate in the negotiations, his presence increased interest in them. After leaving Washington, Kalākaua visited New York and several New England and Midwestern cities before returning to Honolulu on February 15, 1875.

While there was a long delay in ratifying the treaty, it finally took effect on September 9, 1876. The treaty's enactment gave Kalākaua's government a new sense of security. After nearly twenty-five years of persistence, American planters and merchants in Hawaii had a reciprocity treaty which gave Hawaiian sugar preferential treatment over all other foreign sugar. A feverish activity now took place in the expansion of the sugar industry. But the long-term trend favored large, complete plantations that handled all phases of sugar production.

Claus Spreckels

While few American capitalists took advantage of the new opportunities in Hawaii, there was one notable exception — Claus Spreckels, a rich and ruthless California sugar-beet magnate. Beginning in 1876, he started acquiring vast holdings of land on Maui by using various devices from outright purchase and lease to other acts that bordered on blackmail. He also established a shipping line and a bank whose shrewdly placed loans bought the services of the king and many politicians. By 1884, he controlled the entire output of Hawaiian sugar. It wasn't until 1886 that Kalākaua, who had become embarrassed by Spreckels' dictates, managed to float a loan with a London-based syndicate and pay him off, thereby ending his hold on the government.

The prosperity of the plantations created an almost insatiable demand for laborers. This situation, coupled with the decline in the native population, created an urgent need for an increase in Hawaii's population. Yet attempts by both the public and private sectors to encourage emigration from other Pacific islands and other countries were not very successful. Chinese immigrants, on the other hand, flowed steadily into the kingdom. But almost exclusively, only Chinese men could be induced to emigrate from China. Once their contracts were fulfilled, they abandoned the plantations and generally congregated in the towns, again adding to the labor shortages on the plantations.

Japanese Plantation Workers

Beginning in 1878 and continuing for the next ten years, just over 11,000 Portuguese were brought to Hawaii from Madeira and the Azores. But by far the largest immigrant group came from Japan. Japan signed a treaty with Hawaii in late January of 1886 which paved the way for large-scale emigration of Japanese contract laborers to Hawaii. A total of 28,691 Japanese immigrants (including women and children) came to the islands between February of 1885 and June of 1894.

Racial antagonism between native Hawaiians and foreigners intensified during Kalākaua's reign. New leaders in politics and business made their appearance, and many of them had been born in the islands. While Hawaii had no organized political parties until late in Kalākaua's reign, two distinct groups emerged — native Hawaiians and part-Hawaiian's in one group, and haoles (whites) in the other. The rivalry between these groups caused many of the political struggles that plagued Kalākaua's reign.

Walter Murray Gibson

Schemers and adventurers, by playing on Kalākaua's vanity or naivete, could push the king into actions that invited political trouble. One such person was Walter Murray Gibson — an adventurer of dubious character who ran afoul with the founding elders of a Mormon settlement on Lanai. Having acquired a remarkable command of the Hawaiian language, Gibson started a bilingual newspaper which he published in Honolulu. Later, he ran successfully for the legislature. Gradually, he became a power to be reckoned with, and during the power struggle of 1882, the smooth-talking Gibson attained his goal of becoming administrative head of the government. He was now premier and minister of foreign affairs. Between 1882 and 1887, when Kalākaua kept changing his cabinet, Gibson remained.

For some time, Kalākaua had the desire to make a trip around the world — something that no other king had dared. Kalākaua and his party departed Honolulu on January 20, 1881 for San Francisco prior to going first to the Orient and then to Europe. In Italy, the king had an audience with Pope Leo XIII, and in England, he was entertained by Queen Victoria. Kalākaua's European tour afforded him the opportunity to pursue two of his favorite passions — music and military affairs. In the United States, Kalākaua had an interview with President Chester A. Arthur. Traveling across America, the royal party made a number of stops before arriving in San Francisco. The king and his party finally arrived back in Honolulu on October 29, 1881.

Ever since Kalākaua had ascended the throne, he let it be known that he wanted a new palace to match his lofty position as king. He considered the present palace "filthy and in poor condition," and he felt humiliated living in it. The legislative session of 1878 finally authorized the funds for a new palace, and the design was approved in July of the following year. The old palace was razed and the cornerstone for the new palace was laid on December 31, Queen Kapi'olani's birthday. It was completed in the latter part of 1882. (Additional information on 'Iolani Palace appears in chapter 9 of this book.)

Coronation Pavilion and Amphitheater

One of the grandest events of the 1880's was the coronation of King Kalākaua and Queen Kapi'olani on February 12, 1883 — the ninth anniversary of the king's inauguration. Preparations had taken months, and much of the clothing, jewelry, and royal insignia (including two crowns) had been ordered from England and France. A large pavilion[1] was built in front of the palace, and a bridge connected it to the palace's first-floor veranda. A covered amphitheater surrounded the pavilion on three sides and provided seating for several thousand spectators.

Statue of Kamehameha I

The formal investiture presented a mix of ancient-Hawaiian and modern-European pageantry. After receiving his crown from the chancellor of the kingdom, Kalākaua placed it upon his own head and then crowned his queen. The ceremonies included a state dinner and coronation ball at the palace, a regatta, horse races, hula dances, a lū'au, and other entertainment spread over a number of days. The celebration also included the unveiling of a statue of Kamehameha the Great in front of Ali'iōlani Hale on February 14. The statue[2] portrayed Kamehameha as the warrior who united the islands and ushered in a new era of law and peace.

---

[1] Following the coronation, the pavilion was moved to another spot on the palace grounds where it remains today.

[2] The original statue was lost at sea in 1880 near the Falkland Islands. The government ordered a replica and unveiled it in 1883. The original statue was recovered, and it stands in Kohala on the island of Hawaii, Kamehameha's birthplace. A third statue is in the National Statuary Hall in the Rotunda of the Capitol in Washington, D.C. It was unveiled on April 15, 1969.

During Kalākaua's reign, the Royal Hawaiian Band (formed in 1870) became a cultural institution, and Kalākaua encouraged nearly everything musical and dramatic in order to bring gaiety and brightness to Honolulu. Captain Heinrich (Henry) Berger, who led the band since 1872, mastered the Hawaiian language and transcribed countless melodies, chants, and meles (songs). Around 1880, Berger added music to Kalākaua's own composition of "Hawaii Pono'ī" ("Hawaii's Own") which became the national anthem.

Lavish Lū'au at the King's Boathouse

Kalākaua loved the sea and he delighted in the traditions of both paddle and sail craft. He had his own personal boathouse named Healani. Located at Honolulu Harbor, it housed the royal barge and numerous koa-wood racing canoes. Here, Kalākaua escaped the cares of state and often hosted high-stakes poker games or extravagant parties for his tight circle of friends.

Queen Emma, widow of Kamehameha IV, died in April of 1885. Her death was preceded by the deaths of two other important ali'i: Princess Ruth Ke'elikolani in 1883, and Bernice Pauahi Bishop in 1884 - the last two descendants of Kamehameha the Great. Emma's death severed the last link to the Kamehameha dynasty and removed any further threats to the Kalākaua dynasty.

Lack of harmony in Kalākaua's cabinet plus the king's inclination to dismiss his ministers at will and appoint new ones, led to frequent cabinet changes during his seventeen-year reign. These changes made consistent and constructive policy very difficult. In addition, many public-works projects were grossly neglected as funds were channeled into frivolous activities such as maintaining agents in foreign countries, jubilee celebrations[1], excessive military expenditures, a Hawaiian coinage, and various other regal prerogatives.

Opposition to Gibson's administration, fueled by a growing list of scandals and misadventures, grew steadily during late 1886 and early 1887. As demands for reform mounted, the opposition forces united to put an end to the extravagance, corruption, and incompetence of Gibson's administration. This solidarity helped the rapid rise of a secret organization known as the Hawaiian League which, assisted by the Honolulu Rifles, contributed the most to the downfall of Gibson in June of 1887.

The Hawaiian League sought to reform the government by putting a limit on

[1]One such celebration was held on November 16, 1886, the fiftieth anniversary of Kalākaua's birth. It included many of the same types of entertainment that accompanied his coronation.

Jubilee Celebration in Front of 'Iolani Palace (1886)

the king's powers. It wanted him to reign but not to rule which in reality was what he had been doing for the past few years. Threatened by a show of force from the Hawaiian League and unable to get any help from the major powers, Kalākaua agreed to the demands placed upon him. On July 1, he accepted the new cabinet that was thrust upon him. Known as the Reform Cabinet, it quickly produced a new constitution which Kalākaua reluctantly signed after much discussion and open argument with his cabinet. Dubbed the "Bayonet Constitution," it revised the Constitution of 1864, took away the greater part of the king's power, and transferred that power to the cabinet — thereby making the Hawaiian monarch, in effect, a ceremonial figure.

Robert Louis Stevenson at King Kalākaua's Waikiki Beach House

As relations between Kalākaua and his cabinet became severely strained, the king avoided meeting with his ministers as much as possible. To escape embarrassment, Kalākaua spent a great deal of time on the island of Hawaii, and he frequently hosted lū'aus and informal parties for prominent visitors such as Robert Louis Stevenson at his beach house in Waikiki.

Robert W. Wilcox, a part-Hawaiian who had briefly attended a military school in Italy, soon became a prime agitator among the groups that opposed the reform movement. Possessing a magnetic personality, Wilcox formed a secret society in 1889 which sought to restore the government and the king to their former positions and to get rid of the Reform Cabinet. On July 30, Wilcox led an armed, but ill-fated insurrection in which the rebels temporarily occupied the palace grounds and several nearby government buildings. By the time he came to trial, Wilcox had become a hero, and a native jury found him "not guilty" even though sufficient evidence had been presented. Later, the government reduced the height of the masonry wall that surrounded the palace and installed an open iron fence on top of

Robert W. Wilcox

the remaining wall to lessen the danger of a repeat performance.

The Reform Party suffered a major setback in the 1890 election, and a legislative investigation in June caused the ouster of the Reform Cabinet. Happily, Kalākaua appointed a new cabinet which consisted of several of his personal friends. The king and his followers then turned their attention to getting rid of the "Bayonet Constitution." By November, all the amendments necessary to correct the major objections to the existing constitution had passed, and they were scheduled into the 1892 legislative session for final action.

Kalākaua then decided to spend several months on the West Coast in an effort to restore his deteriorating health. Before leaving, he appointed his sister, Princess Lili'uokalani, as regent during his absence. Without fanfare and wearing civilian attire, Kalākaua and a small party left Honolulu on November 25 aboard the *USS Charleston* as guests of Admiral George Brown.

While in California, Kalākaua attended a barrage of balls, receptions, and dinners. In early January of 1891, he suffered a mild stroke while visiting Santa Barbara. He was then taken to San Francisco where a fleet surgeon took personal charge of his case. But despite the best efforts of several doctors, the king's condition worsened, and he lapsed into unconsciousness on the 18th. The final moment came in the afternoon of January 20 when Kalākaua died of Bright's disease at the age of fifty-four.

Kalākaua's Interment at the Royal Mausoleum

Admiral Brown and the *Charleston* returned the king's remains to Honolulu on January 29. Also on that day, Lili'uokalani became the new Hawaiian monarch. Prior to his funeral on February 15, 1891, the king's body was transferred to a new casket fashioned from native Hawaiian woods and adorned with silver and gold decorations. After a religious service in the Throne Room, a long procession escorted the king's coffin through the city streets to the Royal Mausoleum as minute guns were fired by the American warships and by the battery on Punchbowl. Thus the founder of the Kalākaua dynasty was laid to rest in grand ceremonial style, reminiscent of the manner in which he lived.

CHAPTER 8

Queen Lili'uokalani: The Last Monarch

Queen Lili'uokalani and the Hawaiian Throne

John Owen Dominis

LYDIA KAMAKAEHA LILI'UOKALANI
BORN: September 2, 1838
FATHER: Caesar Kapa'akea, son of
Kamanawa II — grand nephew
of Kamanawa I of Kona who
supported Kamehameha I
MOTHER: Keohokalole
RULED: January 29, 1891 until her
overthrow on January 17,
1893. She died on
November 11, 1917.

JOHN OWEN DOMINIS
BORN: March 3, 1832
FATHER: John Dominis, a
prosperous ship captain
from Italy and New England
MOTHER: Mary Lambert Jones
of New York and Boston
DIED: August 27, 1891

Lili'uokalani became queen at the age of fifty-two. Having received her formal education at the Chiefs' Children's School, she spoke English fluently. During her lifetime, Lili'uokalani adhered to the fundamental principles of the Christian religion, much more so than her late brother. She attended church services regularly, and she had a long list of worthy charitable causes. Married since September 16, 1862 to a childhood friend named John Owen Dominis, the queen had no children. Dominis had received an appointment as a full general on the staff of Kamehameha IV, and he later became governor of Oahu under Kamehameha V. The new queen conferred upon her husband the rank and dignity of "His Royal Highness the Prince Consort."

Lili'uokalani visited California in 1878, and in 1887, she toured the United States and England with Queen Kapi'olani. Kalākaua designated her as heir apparent in April of 1877 after the death of her younger brother, Prince William Pitt Leleiohoku. Having served as regent on two occasions during the late king's absence, Lili'uokalani had prepared herself for the duties of sovereign. Proud of her ali'i lineage, the new queen believed in the divine right of an absolute monarch. Spirited and stubborn, yet warm-hearted toward her subjects, she was determined to maintain the traditional prerogatives of the ruling class — prerogatives that her late brother had been forced to relinquish. While the native Hawaiians were filled with hope for change, the haoles were fearful that the new queen would attempt to restore the old constitution and regain the crown's lost power.

Princess Ka'iulani

The new queen quickly appointed a new cabinet more to her own choosing, and she named her niece, Princess Ka'iulani, as heir apparent. Ka'iulani was the daughter of Princess Miriam Likelike, the queen's deceased sister, and Archibald S. Cleghorn. At this time, the fifteen-year-old princess attended a girls' school in England under the guardianship of Theo H. Davies, a family friend who had business interests both in England and Hawaii.

The newspapers of this period cautioned the new queen to accept the modern constitution and reign but not rule. They also warned that the kingdom was slowly going through a period of transition from a monarchy to a democracy. Voices of discord were already being heard from the more radical elements in the community who were isolated from the new administration. During the summer of 1891, the queen's husband became ill, and he died in late August, leaving a vacuum in Lili'uokalani's life during a critical period in her reign.

Sanford B. Dole (left) and Lorrin A. Thurston in Dole's Private Office in His Home

The Reform Party's recent defeat and the subsequent downfall of the Reform Cabinet caused many of the party's supporters to look for other ways to secure good government. One of these ways embraced annexation, and one of the individuals who had changed his mind on the subject was Lorrin A. Thurston. By 1892, he had become an ardent annexationist. Several secret organizations came into existence at this time, and one of them, formed by Thurston, was known as the Annexation Club. Rather than promote annexation outright, the club prepared itself to act quickly should the queen precipitate a crisis by promulgating a new constitution or performing some other absolutist act.

Throughout the spring of 1892, the Liberal Party continued its attacks on the administration and called for the demise of the monarchy. Insurrection rumors became so heavy and frequent that the government placed sandbags around two entrances to the palace — an action which later embarrassed the government. By this time, it had become United States policy to station a warship continuously in Hawaiian waters to support the queen and to aid her government in preserving internal order.

The legislative session of 1892 proved to be the longest one in the kingdom's history. The fiercest and longest battle centered around control of the queen's cabinet. Seven resolutions for "want of confidence" against the cabinet were introduced. Four of them passed, forcing the resignations of four separate cabinets. While the queen exercised her right to appoint her ministers, the legislature kept exercising its right to reject them. The underlying cause of this legislative power struggle was the fact that no party had a majority.

Samuel Parker, Minister of Foreign Affairs

John F. Colburn, Minister of the Interior

William H. Cornwell, Minister of Finance

Arthur P. Peterson, Attorney General

QUEEN LILI'UOKALANI'S LAST CABINET

As rumors of a possible coup d'etat circulated, Lili'uokalani reluctantly compromised with the legislature and accepted a cabinet whose members belonged to the Reform Party. This new cabinet, headed by George N. Wilcox (who was not related to Robert W. Wilcox), consisted of well-known and highly respected members of the community. But as 1892 drew to a close, Lili'uokalani gradually turned against the Wilcox cabinet because of its continued opposition to her proposals. Using her influence in the legislature, the queen forced the resignations of her ministers on January 12. The next day, she appointed a new cabinet and then informed these new ministers of her intention to proclaim a new constitution which would restore power to the crown. But the queen's ministers refused to support her in such a revolutionary act, and they pressured Lili'uokalani into postponing her plans. Reluctantly, the embarrassed queen made an announcement to a group of dignitaries assembled in the Throne Room that she had yielded to her ministers, but that within the near future, she would give them a new constitution.

News quickly spread of the queen's intended action, and a number of disgruntled residents banded together. Inspired by Thurston, who saw an opportunity to promote the views of the Annexation Club, these residents formed a Committee of Safety. All the original members of this thirteen-member committee also belonged to the Annexation Club. During the next two days, the committee took steps to establish and proclaim a Provisional Government. The committee sought

The Committee of Safety[1]

out and was encouraged by the American minister, John L. Stevens. While Stevens took a somewhat neutral stand, he nevertheless stated that he would land American troops to prevent destruction of American lives and property, and that he would recognize the existing government — whichever one controlled the government buildings.

By January 15, 1893, the queen's government knew of the existence of the Committee of Safety and its intended purpose of dethroning the queen. Yet no arrests were made. Reconciliatory attempts by the government came too late to turn back the swelling tide of change that had descended upon the city. Besieged by nervous Americans throughout most of the 16th, Minister Stevens decided to land American troops from the USS Boston. Having instructions to remain neutral, a fully equipped force of 162 Marines and bluejackets descended upon the city.

Caught somewhat by surprise, the queen's ministers protested to Stevens who in turn told them to put any complaints in writing. This action may have led some cabinet ministers to conclude that Stevens supported the revolutionists. Overwhelmed by exaggerated reports on the strength of the opposition and complacent because of the presence of the American troops, Lili'uokalani's cabinet did nothing.

That evening, the Committee of Safety named an advisory and an executive council for its new government. It also asked Sanford B. Dole, an associate justice of the Hawaiian Supreme Court, to serve as president of the executive council. Dole pondered the offer overnight and then accepted it the next morning. The Committee of Safety then took over the government building without any resistance. It

---

[1] The original Committee of Safety consisted of Henry E. Cooper (chairman), Henry Waterhouse, Lorrin A. Thurston, H.F. Glade (replaced by Ed Suhr, pictured above), F.W. McChesney, Albert S. Wilcox (replaced by John Emmeluth, pictured above), William R. Castle, William O. Smith, John A. McCandless, C. Bolte, William C. Wilder, Andrew Brown, and Theodore F. Lansing. Within a day or two, Wilcox resigned to return to Kauai and Glade resigned because he was German consul. The majority of the members were either Americans, Hawaiian born of American parents, or naturalized Hawaiian citizens.

American Minister John L. Stevens

issued a long proclamation which denounced the excesses and unkept promises of the Kalākaua regime and the attempts of Queen Lili'uokalani to restore royal prerogatives and reduce popular rights. Stating that responsible government was impossible under the monarchy, the proclamation abrogated the monarchy, deposed the queen, ousted her ministers, and established a Provisional Government which would seek a union with the United States. With a strong, armed force now mobilized, the new government declared martial law. By five o'clock on the 17th, Stevens had recognized the Provisional Government as the "de facto" government of Hawaii.

The four ousted ministers returned to the palace and advised the queen to surrender to the superior forces of the opposition and not risk bloodshed. Under "protest," she yielded instead to the superior forces of the United States in the hope that she would be reinstated later. She then retired to her private residence to await a favorable decision from the United States.

That evening, under orders from the queen, the police station and its "army" of 272 men surrendered to the Provisional Government which lost no time in having itself recognized and defended. It sent a delegation to Washington to negotiate a treaty uniting Hawaii with the United States; it disbanded the Royal Household Guards; it activated the Hawaii National Guard until a new police force could be installed; and it required all government officials still in office to swear an oath of allegiance. By January 19, it was recognized by all the foreign governments having diplomatic or consular representatives in Hawaii. In an attempt to avoid civil disorder, the American flag was temporarily raised over the government building on February 1, and Stevens placed the government under the protection of the United States while the annexation negotiations continued.

In Washington, the annexation issue became a political football as the Cleveland administration came into power. President Cleveland then sent a special commissioner to investigate the Hawaiian question. Four months later, the tight-lipped special commissioner, James H. Blount, departed Honolulu on August 9 and returned to Washington. Based on his slanted report, the Cleveland administration sought to reinstate Lili'uokalani on the condition that she grant full amnesty to all those who had participated in the revolution.

In November of 1893, a new minister to Hawaii met with the queen and sought out her views on the amnesty issue. Learning that Lili'uokalani remained steadfast in her determination to punish the revolutionists, the American minister, Albert S. Willis, wrote to Washington for new instructions. The United States soon found itself in an awkward position. It could not use force against a government that it and other foreign governments had recognized. So the administration dropped the entire matter in Congress' lap in January of 1894. In the end, the House censured Stevens, but no further action was taken against Hawaii's Provisional Government.

Still intent on annexation, the Provisional Government decided to hang on by forming a republic on July 4, 1894. But in reality, it was the same government with the same people running it. When President Cleveland recognized the Republic of Hawaii, the Royalists were finally convinced that they would have to proceed on their own in restoring their queen to power. But an attempted insurrection in early January of 1895 was a disastrous failure, and it enabled the government to arrest Lili'uokalani on January 16 and imprison her in her own palace!

Pressured by government officials and her supporters, Queen Lili'uokalani signed an abdication document on January 24, forever renouncing her throne and the Hawaiian monarchy. In it, she also recognized the Republic of Hawaii as the only lawful government of Hawaii, and she sought clemency for all her subjects who were involved in the rebellion. Finally, she vowed to live in privacy and retirement from all publicity, and she pledged an oath of allegiance to the republic.

But the republic did not exempt Lili'uokalani from personal liability for her complicity in the revolution. So it kept her under arrest, and in early February, the military court brought her to trial. The initial charge of treason was changed to misprision of treason, that is, concealing knowledge of treason without actually participating in the act. In a trial that lasted several days, the prosecution presented damaging evidence which strongly suggested that she knew what was going on. In the end, the court found her guilty and imposed the maximum sentence — a

$5,000 fine and five years at hard labor! Shortly after the humiliated ex-queen returned to her second-floor "jail cell," Dole remitted the hard-labor portion of her sentence.

Lili'uokalani at Her Private Residence (Washington Place)[1] in the Summer of 1895

In September of 1895, the government granted conditional pardons to Lili'uo-kalani, her nephew (Prince Kūhiō), and many other Royalists. By January 1, 1896, the remaining insurgents were released. In addition, the government relieved Lili'uo-kalani and the others from paying their fines. Eventually, she received an absolute pardon and complete restoration of her civil rights. In December of 1896, she sailed to the United States and remained there until the summer of 1898. During this time, Lili'uokalani lobbied against annexation and wrote her memoirs with the help of Captain Julius A. Palmer, a Bostonian. The book, "Hawaii's Story by Hawaii's Queen," was published in 1898.

Sailors and Marines From the USS Mohican Preparing to Attend Annexation Ceremonies

Congress continued to drag its feet on the annexation treaty until the Spanish-American war quickly brought the strategic importance of the islands to the attention of the American public. By early July of 1898, the annexation issue had been resolved, and President McKinley signed it into law. After an immigration dispute between Japan and Hawaii was settled, the final transfer of sovereignty took place on August 12, 1898. The two American warships in Honolulu Harbor, the *Philadelphia* and the *Mohican,* sent several detachments of troops ashore to attend the ceremonies and to assure an orderly transition.

---

[1]Washington Place, located across Beretania Street from the State Capitol, is the current residence of Hawaii's governor.

As the band played "The Star Spangled Banner," the American flag rose to its prominent position atop the executive building. Like it or not, the Hawaiians had become American citizens. Dole continued to lead the government, only this time as governor-designate of the Territory of Hawaii until Congress proclaimed a formal government. Lili'uokalani, Kapi'olani, Ka'iulani, and other prominent ali'i had been invited to the ceremonies, but none of them attended. Instead most of them gathered at Lili'uokalani's residence and consoled the deposed queen. For them, it was the saddest day in memory. Lili'uokalani's immortal song, "Aloha 'Oe" ("Farewell to Thee"), would have seemed appropriate at this somber gathering.

For the next two decades, Lili'uokalani lived a quiet life at her private residence (Washington Place). The legislature provided her with an annual pension, and she received additional income from a sugar plantation. Time gradually mellowed her bitterness toward her usurpers. When the United States entered World War I, she raised the American flag over her residence for the first time, thereby announcing her loyalty to the United States. After suffering a stroke, Lili'uokalani died on November 11, 1917 at the age of seventy-nine. Her will established the Lili'uokalani Trust for the benefit of orphaned and destitute children of Hawaiian ancestry.

CHAPTER 9

Palaces¹ of the Hawaiian Kingdom·

Early Hawaiian palaces were seldom more than glorified, thatched huts. In most cases, the hut consisted of one large room with no partitions or chambers. Furnishings were simple and few in number. Large woven mats often covered the floor. The residences of high-ranking chiefs consisted of large compounds that might contain six or more separate buildings which were often surrounded by a fence or stone wall. The structures might have included a temple (heiau); a men's eating house (mua); a women's eating house (hale 'aina); a sleeping house (hale noa); a menstrual house (hale pe'a); a work house (hale kua or hale kuku) where the women made kapa (bark cloth); a canoe house (hālau wa'a); and a storehouse (hale papa'a or hale ho'āhu). A chief who ruled over an island might have a very large mua which would also serve as an audience chamber or reception hall — the "palace" to Westerners.

Palace of Kamehameha III in 1826

Kamehameha I and II frequently moved around their kingdom, so they didn't have one official palace. After conquering Oahu, Kamehameha I gradually moved his capital from Hawaii to Oahu. But before settling at Waikiki, he spent about a year in Lahaina, Maui where he occupied an adobe-brick "palace" that had been built by two foreigners for his favorite wife, Ka'ahumanu. In 1809, he moved to a larger compound near Honolulu Harbor. The mua was the largest building in this compound, and it served as the king's palace. The king flew the British flag in front of this building which he called Halehui. A battery of sixteen guns guarded its seaward side. In 1812, Kamehameha returned to the Kona District of Hawaii, and in 1813, he moved across Kailua Bay to Kamakahonu where he spent his last days. Today, the King Kamehameha Hotel and a restored heiau occupy this site.

¹Additional photographs of 'Iolani Palace, Hulihe'e Palace, and The Queen Emma Summer Palace appear in the color centerspread of this publication.

The most permanent palace used by Kamehameha II was known as Pākākā. Located near his father's former palace in Honolulu, it was used from 1821 until the king's death in 1824. Kamehameha III's first royal residence was built near the outskirts of town toward Punchbowl. Known as Haleuluhe, it was used by the young king until around 1836. Then, from about 1836 to about 1840, Halekauwila, near Honolulu Fort, served as the royal abode.

The First 'Iolani Palace

By the 1840's Lahaina had become the center of royal authority, and Kamehameha III spent a great deal of time there. A second palace, known as Hale Piula (House of the Tin Roof), was under construction in Lahaina, but it wasn't completed until the 1850's. It was demolished after high winds caused extensive damage to it in February of 1858. Gradually, Honolulu became the kingdom's commercial center, and Kamehameha III moved the seat of government there. In early February of 1845, the king took up residence in a large coral-block house that had been built by Governor Kekūanaō'a for his daughter, Princess Victoria Kamāmalu.

Initially called Hale Ali'i (House of the Chief), this palace later became known as 'Iolani Palace (Palace of the Bird of Heaven). An eight-foot-high, coral-block wall surrounded the grounds. Four gates provided access to the palace, and each had a distinctive name and purpose. The Kauikeaouli gate was used for state ceremonies; tradesmen used the Kīna'u gate; retainers used the Hakaleleponi gate; and the Likelike gate provided private access for royalty. The first 'Iolani Palace served as the permanent residence for Kamehameha III, IV, and V, Lunalilo, and for part of Kalākaua's reign. Over the years, the grounds were expanded so that other structures could be built nearby.

Kamehameha V undertook an ambitious building program during his reign, and one of his pet projects was the construction of a new palace. But various circumstances, including insufficient finances, delayed the project and changed its initial purpose. Ali'iōlani Hale (House of the Chief unto Heaven) was completed in 1874, and it became a government office building. Known as the Judiciary Building today, it is located on King Street across from the present 'Iolani Palace.

Shortly after Kalākaua ascended the throne, he wanted a new palace to match his new regal position. In 1878, the legislature finally authorized $50,000 for a new palace. Its design, prepared by Thomas J. Baker of Honolulu, was approved in July of the following year. The old 'Iolani Palace was razed, and the cornerstone for the new palace was laid on December 31, 1879.

Completed in the latter part of 1882, the new 'Iolani Palace was constructed of plastered brick and iron with concrete-block trimmings. Its exterior was finished in a light-colored, sanded paint. The 140 by 100 foot palace consists of two stories plus an attic and a cellar, and it is topped off by six towers. A trench, approximately six-feet wide, surrounds the palace to give light and ventilation to the basement.

'Iolani Palace in the 1880's[1]

A wide hall with a massive, hand-carved wooden staircase greets the visitor at the main entrance. The Throne Room, once the scene of royal audiences, balls, and receptions, is located to the right on the main floor. The Blue Room, where informal audiences and small receptions once took place, and the State Dining Room are located across the hall on the left. The queen's bedroom, two guest rooms, the king's bedroom, a library, and the Gold or Music Room are located on the second floor. Originally, the basement contained the chamberlain's apartments, a workshop, a billiard room, and a kitchen.

The 'Iolani Palace Throne Room Around 1890

Due in large part to Kalākaua's demands for regal splendor, the completed palace cost almost $360,000. It's interior was finished in various Hawaiian woods as well as in American walnut and Oregon white cedar. A formal opening banquet was held for the Masonic fraternity on December 27, 1882 followed by a "Grand Open-

[1] The Bungalow (Hale'Ākala) appears to the left of the palace in this photograph. It served as the royal abode until the new palace was completed. It was razed in 1919. The restored and relocated 'Iolani Barracks, only partly visible to the right of the palace, now occupies the Bungalow site.

ing" and coronation ceremony in February of 1883. Originally illuminated by gaslight, the palace was converted to electric light in the summer of 1887. The coral-block wall that surrounded the palace was lowered to approximately three and one-half feet after the Wilcox rebellion of 1889. Two years later, the present iron fence was added. It has since been repainted in its original colors of dark green with gold-tipped pickets.

Following the overthrow of Lili'uokalani in 1893, 'Iolani Palace became informally known as the "Executive Building." It served as the seat of government for the Provisional Government, the Republic of Hawaii, the Territory of Hawaii, and the State of Hawaii. The state government vacated the palace when its new capitol was completed in 1969.

Junior League volunteers initiated the task of restoring the palace to its original grandeur. In March of 1969, The Friends of 'Iolani Palace began supervising the palace's restoration under a contract with the State of Hawaii. Funded by state, federal, and private grants, the restoration required a major reconstruction since the building was leaning several inches forward, termites had ravaged many walls and wooden supports, and rust and peeling paint seemed to be everywhere. The towers, for example, were removed by a crane, completely rebuilt around steel supports, and then rehoisted atop the palace.

Meticulously striving for authenticity, The Friends searched through old records and photographs and hunted down many palace furnishings that had been sold or given away years ago. While some items have been donated, most others had to be repurchased. The multimillion-dollar reconstruction was completed on March 31, 1978, and public tours began in early May of that year. Yet the work of acquiring original palace items continues under the watchful eye of President Abigail Kekaulike Kawānanakoa, grand-daughter of Prince David Kawānanakoa who had been proclaimed a prince of the realm by King Kalākaua in 1883.

The Daughters of Hawaii, a private, historical preservation organization founded in 1903, has taken into its protection the two remaining palaces in Hawaii — Hulihe'e Palace and The Queen Emma Summer Palace. Hulihe'e Palace, built in 1837 - 1838 by Governor Kuakini, is located in Kailua-Kona on the island of Hawaii. It provided tranquility and a place of refuge for many of Hawaii's monarchs. When Queen Kapi'olani died in 1899, her two nephews (David Kawānanakoa and Jonah Kūhiō Kalaniana'ole) inherited the palace. Gradually, the palace fell into disuse, its furnishings were disposed of, and its grounds became a semiwilderness. In 1924, the Daughters of Hawaii set out to save the palace. The Territory of Hawaii acquired the property in 1925 and turned it over to the Daughters in 1927. After being restored, Hulihe'e Palace opened as a museum in 1928.

Located in Oahu's Nu'uanu Valley, The Queen Emma Summer Palace was originally built in the late 1840's as an expensive home for a part Hawaiian named John G. Lewis. John Young II (Keoni Ana) purchased the estate in 1850 and called it Hānaiakamalama ("the foster child of the light (or moon)") after his family's favorite spot at Kawaihae on the island of Hawaii. He died in 1857 and left the estate to his niece, Emma Rooke. Queen Emma and her husband, Kamehameha IV, used the house to escape the hot summer weather. In 1869, Emma had a large room added in the rear of the house in anticipation of giving a party for the Duke of Edinburgh. Although no accounts exist of such a party, the Edinburgh Room was used for entertaining other dignitaries. After Emma's death in 1885, the house was uninhabited until the Hawaiian Monarchical Government purchased the property in 1890. Facing demolition in 1913, the house was saved through the intervention of the Daughters of Hawaii who were granted use of the house as long as they maintained it as a museum. After conducting many fundraising events, the Daughters of Hawaii restored the palace to its former charm and beauty.

CHAPTER 10

Monarchial Burial Sites

Early Hawaiians usually buried their dead in caves or interred them in the sand along the seashore. The bodies were wrapped in kapa (bark cloth) and often tied so that the knees touched the chest. Burials with the body in a prone position, while not uncommon, didn't become common practice until the influence of foreigners and the teachings of the missionaries began to change the customs and attitudes of the Hawaiian people.

But the Hawaiians treated the remains of royalty in a completely different way. After being wrapped in large leaves (such as banana, taro, etc.), the body of a high-ranking chief was temporarily placed in a shallow grave. A fire usually burned continuously over the site for a number of days to aid in the decomposition of the body. Then the remains were removed from the grave, and the bones were cleaned, arranged in their proper order, and wrapped in kapa. The remaining fleshy residue was cast into the ocean during a sacred nighttime ceremony. After a kahuna (priest) had deified the bones, a sennit casket was woven around them, and they were hidden in a secret cave or placed in a sanctuary house to prevent their desecration.

Reconstructed Hale o Keawe Temple at the Pu'uhonua o Hōnaunau National Historical Park

Photo by Author

The bones of Kamehameha the Great were hidden in a cave in this traditional way, and to this day, they have never been found. When Kamehameha II abolished the kapu (tabu) system in 1819, the people were prohibited from worshiping the old gods, and many of their idols and temples were destroyed. Likewise, many of the sanctuary houses met a similar fate. But several royal burial depositories on the island of Hawaii survived for a time, including Hale o Līloa in Waipi'o Valley and Hale o Keawe which was located in a corner of the large pu'uhonua (place of refuge) at Hōnaunau. The remains of several dozen distinguished high chiefs were eventually brought to Honolulu around 1858 and either placed inside the Royal Tomb (located on the grounds of the first 'Iolani Palace) or buried alongside the tomb.

The need for a Royal Tomb arose in 1825 when the bodies of Kamehameha II and Queen Kamāmalu were returned to Honolulu from England aboard the British frigate *Blonde*. They had died of measles the year before while visiting London. After religious services were conducted at Kawaiaha'o Church, their bodies were stored temporarily in Prime Minister Kalanimoku's house until the Royal Tomb could be completed. This ten-foot-high, single-chamber structure had coral-block walls and measured 14 by 18 feet. Several decades later, the tomb held so many coffins that they had to be stacked on koa-wood frames.

Following the death of Kamehameha IV in 1863, construction began on the Royal Mausoleum. Built in the form of a cross, it is located in Nu'uanu Valley several miles north of downtown Honolulu. Workmen completed the west wing of this Gothic-style tomb in January of 1864, and the following month, the bodies of the deceased king and his only son (who died in 1862) were laid to rest there. Construction ceased on the mausoleum while the kingdom observed a year of mourning, and the other three wings were finally completed in the fall of 1865. During the evening of October 30, most of the coffins from the Royal Tomb were moved to the new mausoleum in a somber, torch-lit procession that included militia companies in full-dress uniforms. In May of 1866, the remains of John Young and several members of his family were moved to a grave near the Royal Mausoleum. (Young had been an advisor to Kamehameha I.) Later, the government demolished the Royal Tomb. A grassy mound, enclosed by a low fence, now marks the site of the Royal Tomb on the grounds of 'Iolani Palace.

The Royal Mausoleum in Nu'uanu Valley[1]

Photo by Author

[1] A twenty-three-foot marble shaft on the left marks the site of the Kalākaua Tomb. A flight of stairs leads to the vault below.

The bodies of King Kalākaua and members of his family were also placed in the Royal Mausoleum. In November of 1887, caskets from the Kamehameha dynasty were moved to a separate underground vault nearby. Known as the Kamehameha Tomb, it had been built by Charles R. Bishop after the death of his wife, Bernice Pauahi. The mausoleum underwent a renovation in 1904, and in June of that year, the caskets of nine people who had close connections with the Kamehameha family were placed in the Wyllie Tomb. In June of 1910, caskets of the Kalākaua dynasty were moved to their own separate tomb near the original mausoleum.

Following the death of Bishop in 1915, his ashes were placed next to his wife's casket, and workmen permanently sealed the Kamehameha Tomb. A separate headstone honors the memory of Mr. Bishop. When Queen Lili'uokalani died in 1917, her remains joined those of her relatives in the Kalākaua Tomb. The original mausoleum building became vacant in 1918 when the Bishop Museum received custody to the remains of the ancient chiefs Līloa and Lonoikamakahiki. In 1922, this building was converted into a chapel, and a small koa-wood altar was erected in the east wing. The altar bears the inscription "Hemolele, Hemolele, Hemolele" ("Holy, Holy, Holy"). Since 1948, this sacred cemetery has been open to the public.

The Lunalilo Mausoleum [1]

Yet the remains of one recent monarch are not in the Royal Mausoleum. Having felt slighted by the clannish Kamehameha family, King Lunalilo's last wish was to be buried away from them. The Royal Mausoleum temporarily housed his casket until the Lunalilo Tomb was sufficiently completed in late 1875. Located in a corner of the cemetery at the entrance to Kawaiaha'o Church, the Lunalilo Mausoleum, with the remains of his family nearby, stands aloof to the remnants of the other reigning monarchs in the Royal Mausoleum.

[1]The inscription "Lunalilo Ka Mō'ī" above the entrance means "Lunalilo the King."

Selected Bibliography

Alexander, William D. *History of Later Years of the Hawaiian Monarchy and the Revolution of 1893.* Honolulu: Hawaiian Gazette Co., 1896.

Bailey, Paul. *Those Kings and Queens of Old Hawaii.* Los Angeles: Westernlore Books, 1975.

Bingham, Hiram. *A Residence of Twenty-One Years in the Sandwich Islands.* New York: Praeger Publishers, 1969 (Reprint of the 1855 third and final edition).

Daws, Gavan. *Shoal of Time; A History of the Hawaiian Islands.* New York: The MacMillan Co., 1968.

Day, A. Grove. *History Makers of Hawaii.* Honolulu: Mutual Publishing of Honolulu, 1984.

Day, A. Grove. *Kamehameha, First King of Hawaii.* Honolulu: Hogarth Press, 1974.

Dole, Sanford B. *Memoirs of the Hawaiian Revolution.* Honolulu: Advertiser Publishing Co., Ltd., 1936.

Dutton, Meiric K. *Hawaii's Great Seal and Coat of Arms.* Honolulu: Loomis House Press, 1960.

Feher, Joseph. *Hawaii: A Pictorial History.* Honolulu: Bishop Museum Press, 1969.

Hawaii, University of — College of Arts and Sciences, Dept. of Geography. *Atlas of Hawaii.* Honolulu: University Press of Hawaii, 1973.

Joesting, Edward. *Hawaii; An Uncommon History.* New York: W.W. Norton & Co., Inc., 1972.

Judd, Walter F. *Palaces and Forts of the Hawaiian Kingdom: From Thatch to American Florentine.* Palo Alto, Cal.: Pacific Books, 1975.

Kamakau, Samuel M. *Ruling Chiefs of Hawaii.* Honolulu: The Kamehameha Schools Press, 1961.

Kuykendall, Ralph S. *The Hawaiian Kingdom. Vol. I, 1778—1854, Foundation and Transformation; Vol. II, 1854—1874, Twenty Critical Years; Vol. III, 1874—1893, The Kalakaua Dynasty.* Honolulu: University of Hawaii Press, Vol. I, 1938; Vol. II, 1953; Vol. III, 1967.

Liliuokalani. *Hawaii's Story by Hawaii's Queen.* Rutland, Vt.: Charles E. Tuttle Co., 1964 (Reprint of the 1898 edition).

Malo, David. *Hawaiian Antiquities (Moolelo Hawaii).* Honolulu: Bishop Museum Press, 1951.

Mellen, Kathleen D. *An Island Kingdom Passes.* New York: Hastings House, 1958.

Peterson, Barbara Bennett. (Editor). *Notable Women of Hawaii.* Honolulu: University of Hawaii Press, 1984.

Pukui, Mary Kawena & Elbert, Samuel H. *Hawaiian Dictionary: Hawaiian-English/ English-Hawaiian.* Honolulu: University of Hawaii Press, 1984 combined edition.

Rubincam, Milton. *America's Only Royal Family: Genealogy of the Former Hawaiian Ruling House.* National Genealogical Society Quarterly, Vol. 50, June 1962, pp. 79—91.

Schmitt, Robert C. *Demographic Statistics of Hawaii, 1778—1965.* Honolulu: University of Hawaii Press, 1968.

Swenson, J. Patricia Morgan & Midkiff, Evanita S. *Treasures of the Hawaiian Kingdom.* Honolulu: Daughters of Hawaii, 1984.

Tate, Merze. *The United States and the Hawaiian Kingdom (A Political History).* New Haven, Conn.: Yale University Press, 1965.

Thurston, Lorrin A. *Memoirs of the Hawaiian Revolution.* Honolulu: Advertiser Publishing Co., Ltd., 1936.

Towse, E. *The Rebellion of 1895.* Honolulu: Hawaiian Star, 1895.

Tregaskis, Richard W. *The Warrior King: Hawaii's Kamehameha the Great.* New York: MacMillan Publishing Co., Inc., 1973.

Williams, Edith B. *Ka Hae Hawaii (The Hawaiian Flag); The Story of the Hawaiian Flag.* Honolulu: South Seas Sales, 1963.